The

How to Profit

Blue Way

by Investing in a Better World

Daniel de Faro Adamson
and Joe Andrew

Simon & Schuster Paperbacks
NEW YORK   LONDON   TORONTO   SYDNEY

Simon & Schuster Paperbacks
1230 Avenue of the Americas
New York, NY 10020

First Simon & Schuster trade paperback edition September 2008

SIMON & SCHUSTER PAPERBACKS and colophon are registered trademarks
of Simon & Schuster, Inc.

For information about special discounts for bulk purchases,
please contact Simon & Schuster Special Sales at 1-800-456-6798
or business@simonandschuster.com.

Book text designed by Paul Dippolito

Manufactured in the United States of America

10   9   8   7   6   5   4   3   2   1

The Library of Congress cataloged the hardcover edition as follows:
 Adamson, Daniel de Faro
     The blue way : how to profit by investing in a better world / Daniel de Faro
 Adamson and Joe Andrew
        p.   cm.
 Includes bibliographical references and index.
 1. Investments—Moral and ethical aspects. I. Andrew, Joseph. II. Title.
 HG4515.13.A33   2007
 332.6'042—dc22   2007028175

ISBN-13: 978-1-4165-4734-1
ISBN-10:   1-4165-4734-7
ISBN-13: 978-1-4165-4735-8 (pbk)
ISBN-10:   1-4165-4735-5 (pbk)

To Daniel's mom and dad, Lauren and Wally.

To Joe's mom, Sylvia Hanselmann.

Contents

Contents

PART ONE

The Blue Sector

CHAPTER 1

The Great Illusion

THERE IS A MYTH IN AMERICA THAT VICTORY ON THE great battlefield of capitalism is won by those willing to set ethics aside—by those willing to scorch the earth, put our safety at risk, and squeeze their employees in the name of profit.

Many of us absorb our first, formative business lesson on a grade school playground when we hear "Nice guys finish last." This lesson is echoed over and over by mentors, colleagues, competitors, and even the financial authorities: "Either you can choose to do good or you can choose to make money." Just consider the U.S. Securities and Exchange Commission (SEC), the official standard-bearer of good sense in American financial markets. The SEC requires any mutual fund that invests in ethical companies to disclose this fact—not because the fund deserves special recognition, but, to the contrary, because the SEC views ethical investing *as a risk to investors.*

But what if this cutthroat view of capitalism were really just a myth? What if we could prove—using hard, peer-reviewed data from financial markets—that responsible, progressive corporate leadership doesn't just make a company nicer but makes its shareholders richer? What if progressive values were better, not only for employees, the environment, and our country but for investors and for a company's financial bottom line?

That is precisely what we will describe: an ethical business strategy that we call the *Blue Way*. Conscientious, values-based leadership doesn't just lead to a cleaner environment and more equal opportunity. It also produces greater innovation, prosperity, and success. While this business strategy may sound too good to be true, we believe it is a blueprint for a sweeping progressive revival in which every American can participate. The principles that guide progressive leaders are equally valuable to voters who want to win elections and to investors who want to beat the stock market.

This book marks the first time that anyone has set down the Blue Way in print as a guide for investors, business leaders, concerned citizens, and political organizers. But the Blue Way's basic principles have been intuitively understood by a generation of the most successful, progressive entrepreneurs and CEOs. These visionaries—leaders of what we call "blue companies"—have had the courage to brush aside the conventional wisdom and follow an unpopular but ultimately more rewarding view of economic enterprise.

These blue company leaders have done the hard work for us. They are the ones who have generated the wealth of empirical evidence, from stock market performance data to personal stories and anecdotes, that illustrates the power of the Blue Way. They have put the principles of progressive leadership to the toughest possible test—the test of the free market—and passed with flying colors.

Stock market performance of blue companies compared to red companies and the S&P 500

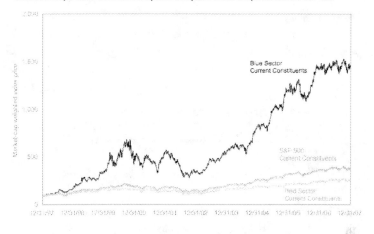

What this chart shows is that not only have blue companies beaten the S&P 500 index, they have done so consistently and dramatically.* We're pretty sure that these results will be just as surprising to most American progressives as to any archconservative ideologue. Progressives are used to hearing that their values and policies will help low-income Americans make it out of poverty, ensure equal protection under the law, or cut air and water pollution—not that they'll help companies dramatically outperform the stock market. Meanwhile, the media machine regularly tars Democrats as "socialists" whose utopian economic views will strangle America's great companies and send the stock market crashing. This smear campaign has had an

---

*Investors should be cautioned that past performance is no guarantee of future results. In addition, the results illustrated are model results, and there are inherent limitations in the use of model results.

impact not only on CEOs and the business press but also on plenty of ordinary progressives who have internalized the idea that their values are bad for business.

If the data above are not astonishing enough already, over the next several chapters we will show that being "blue" has been a better predictor of stock market success than traditional financial metrics, including a strong forward PE ratio and a good dividend yield. Even more striking, this phenomenon is widespread, spanning nearly every segment of the economy from consumer staples to telecommunications to utilities to financial services. Is this "freakonomics"? No, it is the traditional marketplace, where ethical companies are rewarded. *The Blue Way* is a wake-up call: progressives should be proud of their economic record. As we will discuss later, Democratic presidents have been better stewards of the economy over the last century than their Republican counterparts. "Blue" CEOs have on the whole administered better, more successful companies than their conservative counterparts. Core progressive values—equal opportunity, protection of fundamental human rights and freedoms, environmental sustainability, and fair treatment of all citizens regardless of race, gender, class, or orientation—are not only a better basis for running the American economy, they're a better basis for running a business.

One of the great things about *The Blue Way* is that, thanks to the hard data available from financial markets, you don't have to sit back and take our word for it. As you read on, you'll see how anyone with a spreadsheet, Internet access, and a little patience can replicate our work and confirm just how financially successful the "Blue Sector" of consistently progressive companies has been.

Most investors will of course be intensely curious about the specific ways that socially responsible values contribute to corporate success. As we hunted for the distinctive qualities of Blue Sector companies that could plausibly explain their financial outperformance, we discovered that blue company leaders' deeply held values tend to express themselves in what we call the Six Pillars of Progressive Leadership:

- *A culture of innovation.* Blue companies include many of America's most innovative companies—not only technology and Internet firms but companies that set themselves apart from their sector by adopting particularly innovative business strategies.
- *Organizational flexibility.* Blue companies are more likely to experiment with flat, flexible, participatory organization structures that allow good ideas to flow freely from the roots of the organization to the top.
- *Ecoefficiency.* Blue companies have a strong record in improving the efficiency of their energy and natural resource consumption.
- *Investment in employees' well-being.* The Blue Sector includes many of America's most employee-friendly companies, with above-average benefits packages, profit sharing, and strong commitment to employee diversity.
- *Constructive relationships with critics.* Blue companies tend to respond productively to critics and advocacy groups, acknowledging problems and seeking a collaborative response.
- *Long-term perspective.* Blue company leaders display a long-term vision and refuse to get sidetracked or seduced by short-term considerations.

Later in *The Blue Way,* we will explore each of these pillars in greater detail, drawing on the strategies of CEOs who have employed them to maximum effect. We will also see how the lessons of these private-sector progressives are essential in reviving progressive politics.

In fact, politics will be front and center in this book. An investor who wants to get rich the blue way can't just look at the social and environmental behavior of America's biggest companies. Plenty of companies manage to put up a good PR smoke screen or do the minimum necessary to pass various social screens. Those companies have not really internalized socially responsible values, and they don't enjoy the financial benefits that flow from genuine progressive leadership.

Instead, investors need to look critically at companies' demonstrable political behavior. CEOs show their true colors when it comes time to make personal and corporate political contributions. Blue Sector corporations all support Democratic candidates with the majority of their political spending—a practice that flies directly in the face of one of America's most cherished prejudices.

Getting the Blues

The two of us stumbled onto this insight from different sides. For his part, Joe Andrew saw the Blue Sector years before he understood what he was seeing. In 1999, Joe was elected the national chair of the Democratic National Committee (DNC). A successful corporate lawyer and entrepreneur, Joe now turned his attention to being the CEO of the party. One of the national chair's roles is to raise money for the Democrats and oversee how it is spent. As a result, Joe was constantly on the move, visiting CEOs from many of the big companies in America. Joe was no stranger to corporate boardrooms, but what he found surprised even him.

Some of the CEOs were receptive to his requests. Some turned Joe down flat. At first, Joe wondered whether he was a sore loser, because he repeatedly got the feeling that the receptive companies were *better* than the ones that turned him down flat—not just in terms of their values but in terms of their financial success. As time went by, Joe became sure that it wasn't just him: these companies really did tend to be more successful, both in terms of market performance and business ethics.

Of course, as Joe got to know corporate America, he also realized the scale of the Republican fund-raising advantage. Today nearly five times as many of America's richest companies support Republicans as Democrats. More than twice as much corporate money is donated to Republicans than to Democrats. And that's just formal federal political contributions from the companies' political action committees and their senior leadership—it doesn't count the deep, hidden aquifer of corporate capital that nourishes conservative lobbyists, think tanks, university programs, and media. Joe's term as chair of the DNC ended in February 2001, just as George W. Bush began demonstrating the full power of this corporate-fueled Republican machine.

A few years later, Joe was introduced to a young entrepreneur who had also noticed that progressive companies were thriving: Daniel de Faro Adamson. Whereas Joe had observed the Blue Sector from the political side, Daniel came at it from the world of private equity and investment management. Joe had a general impression from observing progressive CEOs in action; Daniel had the numbers to back it up. Joe understood the power of private-sector capital and possessed insights to revitalize the Democratic Party. Daniel, a veteran of Wall Street and McKinsey & Company, understood the potential for progressive investors to beat the market by putting their money into pro-Democratic companies.

Today, we're writing this book to invite every progressive American to consciously take part in the great untold story of the U.S. economy, as well as for every business leader, Democrat or Republican, who would like to use ethical management principles to deliver shareholder value. The Blue Sector has remained unidentified for years. When socially responsible investment became popular, analysts and investors began examining companies' environmental and human rights records but continued to avert their eyes from companies' politics—perhaps feeling that there is something messy or sinister about politics in general. As a result, we believe they missed out on the primary factor that distinguishes companies that have a good "socially responsible" public relations spin from those that benefit from real progressive leadership. We believe, in short, that the analysts and investors missed out on the chance to make the world a better place while also making money.

We are also writing for a new generation of progressive organizations and activists that are unafraid of corporate America. They understand that responsible, progressive corporations are not just a source of political funds but the cornerstone of a thriving, fair, and sustainable economy; they also know that capital is the mother of invention, in politics as in business. Blue CEOs have plenty of lessons for like-minded leaders in the non-profit and government spheres. The traits that make progressives great in the private sector can also contribute to an energetic revival of progressive politics.

The progressive movement needs to reverse the three fundamental advantages that American conservatives have enjoyed for the last few decades. First, the Republicans have the majority of America's big corporations on their side, with all the power, money, and organization that implies. Second, they've channeled their flood of corporate contributions into a highly developed political capital market, which sustains their successful political organizations and fuels a steady succession of promising start-ups. Finally, the conservative movement has outplayed progressives in the game of infrastructure building, setting up a formidable network of right-wing media outlets, think tanks, grassroots mobilization outfits, leadership training institutes, political advocacy groups, and so on.

This thriving political infrastructure—and in particular the sophisticated financial infrastructure that pipes money to all the other bits of the machine—is the seminal reason that the Republicans have been able to shift American politics so far to the right. Their success in institution building has gained them more power than the results of any single election. Despite periodic setbacks like Bill Clinton's victories and the meltdown of the GOP Congress in 2006, the conservative machine will keep coming back stronger unless we can cut off the fuel that sustains it: corporate capital.

The Blue Sector hits the conservative money machine in its ideological foundations by disproving the myth that the new Republicans are the natural party of business. Unfortunately, like most people, corporate bosses would prefer to tune out uncomfortable truths about the need to change their ways. Despite our backgrounds, on the spectrum of people with the power to get CEOs to sit up and pay attention, "a couple of Democrats writing a book" fall somewhere between "the shoeshine guy" and "the intern who makes the coffee." We need to get our message out to the people who can really concentrate minds in corporate America. These people are more influential than members of Congress, or the EPA, the SEC, or even the *Wall Street Journal* editorial board. We're writing to investors and consumers.

If progressive Americans concentrate their support behind the Blue Sector—through their consumer decisions, through shareholder proxy votes, through choosing to invest in progressive companies—we'll be able to divert the largest river of capital that feeds the conservative pool. For that diversion to benefit the progressive movement, though, we need to match the other two conservative advantages: we need to build our own political capital market and a new generation of political infrastructure that adopts the best lessons from the Blue Sector. In the final chapters of this book, we will describe what we've got right now on the Democratic side, and offer a blueprint for all that we still need to develop.

The Blue Way is not just a moneymaking guide. It is also a progressive call to arms. We want to open Americans' eyes to the impact of corporate money on politics. We want to highlight the success of the Blue Sector and demolish the myths that keep American business locked into the Republican camp. At the same time, we want to bring the best lessons from the Blue Sector into progressive politics. The Republican model has faltered, and the progressive movement is searching for a new way forward. There is no better time to pull back the curtain on the powerful but flawed illusions that sustain the conservative money machine. There is no better time to build a new foundation for the progressive movement.

CHAPTER 2

Seeing Red

EVERY TRULY SUCCESSFUL REVOLUTION BECOMES invisible. Whether it's a new technology, a new form of government, or a transformation in lifestyle, after a few years people take it for granted. This kind of revolution is like a tinted window—it colors everything we see, but usually we don't even notice the tint.

The Republican politicization of corporate America is no exception. Over the years, even progressives began tacitly assuming that corporations would have a certain level of Republican bias. As a result, when most Americans hear that on the whole Republicans get more money from business, they shrug. They don't really understand the scale of the money gap between America's political parties, and they certainly don't connect it to their own economic decisions.

If we're going to reverse the trend, progressive consumers and investors need to shed their rose-tinted glasses, see the extraordinary extent to which Republicans dominate the business landscape, and learn to distinguish "red" companies from "blue" companies.

Myth: Basically, the money I spend or invest is politically neutral.

Few investors, and still fewer consumers, think of their money as political. To the extent that they think about it at all, many assume that the money they put into America's biggest companies "all comes out in the wash" politically. After all, even if Republicans are perceived as the more business-friendly party, surely big corporations contribute to both sides. When either political party could win the next election, it wouldn't make sense for companies to put all their eggs in one basket. In any case, what impact can an individual purchase or investment have?

Ironically, while ignoring the political impact of their money, more and more Americans have become concerned with its social and environmental impact. Shoppers have shown a growing demand for organic, fair-trade, and ecofriendly products. Socially responsible investment has boomed over the last thirty-five years. Progressives in particular have demanded that their mutual fund or 401(k) investment dollars go to companies that match their values. Accordingly, there has been a boom in funds that invest only in companies that meet basic progressive criteria: environmental sustainability, fair treatment of all employees, diversity in the workforce and leadership, and respect for human rights.

Of course, a socially and environmentally irresponsible American government can do vastly more harm than an irresponsible company. But because of the myth that investment is politically neutral, not even progressive mutual funds ask whether their "responsible" companies contribute money to an irresponsible political party or government. As a result, their portfolios end up reflecting the bias of the market as a whole.

The bottom line? Progressives may feel good about their decisions to invest in socially responsible funds, but they have unwittingly become owners of the very companies that send millions of dollars to Republican candidates.

> **Reality: Because of the strong political bias of America's top companies, most consumers and investors—even "socially responsible" investors—end up indirectly pouring money into the Republican Party.**

In late October 2006, ABC Radio accidentally let slip an internal memo that demonstrated the political power and bias of corporate America. At least ninety major corporations had quietly insisted that they didn't want their ads run on any programming associated with Air America Radio, the ground-breaking progressive talk radio network.[1] These companies are not apolitical or concerned about their partisan reputation; most of them happily run ads during ABC's conservative shows. The blacklist was aimed very deliberately at the financially troubled flagship of progressive radio. The ninety companies that shunned Air America represent a broad range of national and multinational firms, from Nestlé and Hormel to Bank of America and FedEx.

The overwhelming majority of these companies have one obvious trait in common: they are net contributors to the Republican Party.

Big business wasn't always such an activist, partisan force in American politics. In the wake of the Great Depression, corporate America settled into four decades of off-and-on cooperation with liberal reformers and labor unions. Back in the 1950s and 1960s, businessmen simply didn't behave like a political interest group. Many CEOs established and participated in nonpartisan policy institutes like the Committee for Economic Development, which accepted the need for constructive government interventions in the economy.[2] Even business organizations that were hostile to government regulation, such as the U.S. Chamber of Commerce, were reluctant to engage in direct politicking. They didn't want to become too explicitly partisan.

Today, the U.S. Chamber of Commerce—a body that supposedly represents all American business—is the second largest overt donor to Republican causes. It has become so partisan that even some corporate lobbying groups like the Business Roundtable have distanced themselves from it, claiming to prefer a strategy that is "more measured, less antagonistic, and less confrontational."[3] During the 2004 presidential race, the Chamber poured more than $5.6 million into conservative "527 groups," tax-exempt organizations that are meant in theory to address issues without explicitly advocating the election or defeat of specific candidates.[4] (Under current campaign finance law, 527 groups can still receive unlimited contributions—whether they are long-standing single-issue groups like the National Abortion Rights Action League (NARAL) or the National Rifle Association (NRA), or groups like the anti–John Kerry Swift Boat Veterans, whose only "issue" is intimately related to a specific candidate.) Overall, the Chamber is the top source of conservative lobbying money and the second largest funder of pro-Republican 527 groups.[5]

After the Red Shift

The glaring partisanship of the Chamber of Commerce is just the most obvious sign that corporate America has lost its political compass. The full scale of the problem becomes clear if we look at the political giving of the companies in the Standard & Poor's 500 Composite Stock Price Index (more commonly known as the S&P 500). These five hundred companies make up more than 70 percent of the total market value of all stocks traded in the United States. They're a good proxy for the U.S. stock market in general. And collectively, their political bias is unmistakable.[6]

If you add up all their political spending over the last five congressional election cycles (going back to the last three years of Bill Clinton's presidency), only 16 percent of S&P 500 companies have supported the Democrats with the majority of their

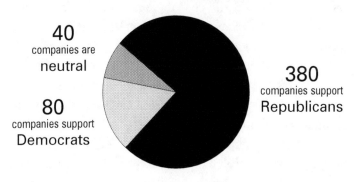

Political Donations of S&P 500 Companies

40 companies are neutral

80 companies support Democrats

380 companies support Republicans

contributions. By contrast, 380 companies (76 percent) have sent most of their contributions to the Republican Party. These companies include not just the "usual suspects" that have hit the headlines for their cozy relationship with the Bush administration (e.g., Enron), but a roster of household names that send more than 80 percent of their political contributions to the GOP. The companies with the strongest pro-Republican slant include:

Tyco International (95%)	Nordstrom (96%)
Circuit City Stores (90%)	The Hershey Company (94%)
Exxon Mobil Corporation (94%)	Campbell Soup (85%)
Halliburton (94%)	Dell (93%)
The Kroger Co. (89%)	Charles Schwab (94%)
Wendy's International (91%)	Safeco Corporation (87%)

This exceptional level of collaboration has yielded striking financial benefits for the Republicans. Over the last decade, the top executive officers and corporate political action committees (PACs) of S&P 500 companies have poured roughly $316 million into American politics. More than two thirds of that money went to the Republican Party.[7]

Nearly the same ratio holds true when you step outside the S&P 500 and look at the contributions of all business-related PACs in the United States.[8]

Not all corporations donate equally, and the real megadonors don't have a political slant so much as a political consensus. Consider the fifty companies whose PACs and top executives donated the most money to political campaigns over the past decade—from Home Depot's relatively modest $1.6 million to AT&T's extravagant $11 million. Collectively, they spent $190 million, almost half of all the formal corporate contributions from

Corporate Political Contributions of S&P 500 Companies

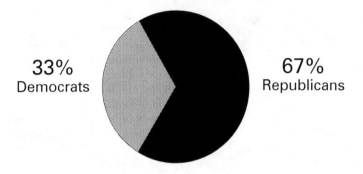

33%
Democrats

67%
Republicans

Political Contributions of Corporate PACs

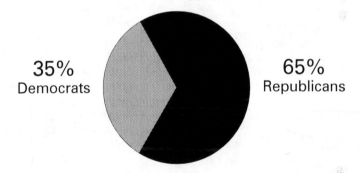

35%
Democrats

65%
Republicans

the S&P 500. And all fifty sent the majority of their money to the Republican Party and its candidates.[9] Not one favored the Democrats in their profligate political spending.

If we had ranked them by the percentage of their contributions rather than alphabetically, it would be obvious that fewer than half of these megadonors are even within 10 percent of being politically neutral. Twenty favor the Republicans, with between 60 percent and 69 percent of their political spending,

Top 50 Corporate Political Donors
in 1998–2008 Election Cycles

Company	% of political contributions to Republicans	Company	% of political contributions to Republicans
Altria Group	68	International Paper	84
American Electric Power	69	Johnson & Johnson	60
Amgen	67	JPMorgan Chase & Co.	59
Anheuser-Busch	57	Lockheed Martin	59
AT&T	58	Merck	68
Bank of America	55	Metlife	54
Boeing Company	59	Microsoft Corporation	56
Burlington Northern Santa Fe	67	Morgan Stanley	62
Chevron	81	Northrop Grumman	63
Chicago Mercantile Exchange	58	Pfizer	68
CIGNA	84	Raytheon	58
Citigroup	59	Sprint Nextel	59
Comcast	52	Textron	67
Edison International	56	Time Warner	54
El Paso	77	Tyson Foods	60
Eli Lilly	71	U.S. Bancorp	67
Exelon	56	Union Pacific	80
Exxon Mobil	93	United Parcel Service	69
Ford Motor	76	United Technologies	63
General Dynamics	61	Valero Energy	81
General Electric	59	Verizon Communications	66
General Motors	70	Wachovia	69
Goldman Sachs Group	58	Wal-Mart Stores	74
Home Depot	67	Washington Mutual	55
Honeywell International	61	Wells Fargo	60

and the remaining eleven companies have given between 70 percent and 94 percent of their multimillion-dollar contributions to the Republican party.

Of course, corporate America's political spending goes far beyond overt contributions to political parties. Big corporations and the foundations attached to them have put millions of dollars directly into conservative advocacy groups, university pro-grams, and think tanks. (The Wal-Mart Foundation, for example, has consistently supported conservative educational groups with its grant program.)[10] And the real money is in lobbying. In 2004, lobbyists spent $2.16 billion to influence government deci-sions, up from $1.45 billion in 1999.[11] Federal lobbying was not always a wildly partisan activity—smart corporate lobbyists used to want friends on both sides of the aisle—but the twelve-year-long Republican control of Congress saw the rise (and fall) of the most ideological lobbying machine in American history.

When the Republicans first took both houses of Congress in 1994, they were determined to dominate lobbying dollars as thor-oughly as they dominated corporate PAC contributions. Their highly effective campaign was known as the "K Street Project," named after the epicenter of Washington's lobbying industry.[12] Republican lawmakers led by former Representative Tom DeLay and former Senator Rick Santorum and strategists led by the anti-tax ideologue Grover Norquist informed lobbyists that the price of access to Congress was wholehearted support of the Republican Party. They built a database of individual lobbyists, focusing on their political contributions and party allegiance, and bullied K Street firms to sack Democrats and promote Republicans. Ultra-partisan lobbyists like the now-infamous Jack Abramoff put added pressure on their colleagues to hew to the GOP line.

Organizations that ignored this ultimatum were explicitly

penalized, as when the Motion Picture Association of America had $1.5 billion in tax breaks written out of a pending bill, allegedly for the offense of hiring Dan Glickman, a former Clinton administration secretary of agriculture, as head of its lobbying effort.[13] The Republicans held up the MPAA example to intimidate other lobbyists and corporations who were seen as disloyal. In the 2004 election cycle, for instance, BlueCross BlueShield Association dared to contribute more to Democrats than to Republicans. BlueCross is (ironically) a deep red association, which had reliably sent its money to the GOP for the previous three cycles. The Republicans erupted in outrage and publicly threatened to punish BlueCross for its effrontery. Grover Norquist, head of the K Street Project, fumed, "This is inexplicable. Are they jealous of Dan Glickman?"[14] In the 2006 election cycle, a chastened BlueCross returned to the fold, sending 56 percent of its PAC contributions to Republican candidates.[15] With that sort of browbeating by the majority party, it's a wonder that any of America's big companies stuck with the Democrats.

Thanks to the sticks and carrots doled out by DeLay, Norquist, and company, K Street became populated not by corporate lobbyists who happened to be Republican but by ideological conservatives who could be counted on to support a right-wing social and economic agenda while raising even more money for Republican candidates. These loyal lobbyists and the corporate interests behind them were given extraordinary influence over the lawmaking process, actually writing key energy and pharmaceutical legislation. At the same time, lobbyists were also expected to take on roles as fund-raisers and ideological enforcers.

The close embrace was bound to lead to corruption, especially after the Republicans fought against tightening the rules on gifts from lobbyists to legislators. One by one many of the main participants in the Republican corporate-political machine fell to scandal—companies like Enron (with its roughly $2 million annual lobbying budget),[16] members of Congress like DeLay, influence peddlers like Abramoff. Yet conservative lawmakers quashed any serious attempt to reform the lobbying system until November 7, 2006, when the persistent sleaze claimed another well-deserved casualty: the Republican Congress. It remains to be seen if the discredited right-wing lobbying machine will fall apart along with its congressional masters or survive on the strength of billions of corporate dollars.

Investing in the Right

Wall Street has generally marched to the same drummer as the rest of corporate America. Between 1994 and 2004, the securities and investment industry consistently sent between 52 and 58 percent of its political donations to the Republicans.[17] In the 2004 election cycle, that amounted to more than $48 million.

This helps explain one reason why the Bush administration pushed so hard (if ultimately in vain) for Social Security privatization—that is, for moving retirement benefits money out of a government trust fund and into private money management. Big government programs don't provide campaign contributions to the Republican Party; private mutual funds do.[18] And thanks to the "red shift" in American business, even investment funds that don't contribute directly to Republicans contribute *indirectly* through the companies in their portfolios.

Just look at where the ten biggest U.S.-based large-cap funds are putting most of their money. In our survey of the top 25 holdings in these mutual funds, we found that 79 percent were com-

Top 25 Holdings of 10 Largest U.S. Large-Cap Mutual Funds

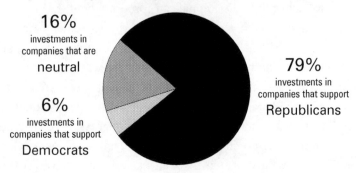

16%
investments in
companies that are
neutral

79%
investments in
companies that support
Republicans

6%
investments in
companies that support
Democrats

Top 25 Holdings of 10 Largest SRI Mutual Funds

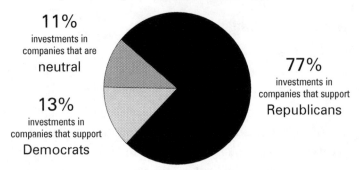

11%
investments in
companies that are
neutral

77%
investments in
companies that support
Republicans

13%
investments in
companies that support
Democrats

panies that favored the Republicans, 6 percent favored the Democrats and 16 percent were neutral—a distribution even more politically skewed than the market as a whole. (Percentages are rounded to the nearest percent.)

Sadly and surprisingly, the same is currently true in the socially responsible investment industry. We ran the same survey for ten of the largest large-cap socially responsible funds in the U.S. Of their top 25 holdings, 77 percent leaned Republican, 13 percent leaned Democrat, and 11 percent were neutral.

Additionally, even many billion-dollar socially responsible funds have achieved a great deal by refusing to invest in major polluters or companies with a poor human rights record abroad. But by averting their eyes from the politics of the companies in their portfolio, even the big progressive funds have ended up dominated by strongly red companies, including:

Illinois Tool Works (97%)	Home Depot (75%)
Motorola (68%)	Procter & Gamble (78%)
Medtronic (81%)	EOG Resources (97%)
PepsiCo (74%)	Johnson & Johnson (62%)
Intel Corporation (79%)	Amgen (72%)
Wells Fargo (62%)	

How on earth has corporate America gotten so skewed that even "progressive" mutual funds end up sending money to the Republican Party? It would make perfect sense if Republicans really were better for business or if pro-Republican companies tended to outperform the market, but as we will see, that's just not true.

Rather, conservative ideologues have sold corporate America a bill of goods—beginning with a little-known memorandum that inspired key right-wing institutions and presciently called for corporate America to get political. It took the conservatives more than three decades to mobilize money behind their ideology, win over corporate America, and move on to conquer Washington. Coincidentally, over the exact same period, progressives have been developing the tool kit of socially responsible investment—investment tools that not only make the world a better place but also offer us a chance to puncture the Republican machine's fuel tank.

The Red Herring and the Manifesto

No one knew it at the time, but two movements that would transform Wall Street were launched within weeks of each other in August 1971. The first movement wanted to mobilize American business behind socially responsible ideals. The second wanted to mobilize American business behind a conservative political machine. Both movements began with simple, relatively short documents: a prospectus and a memorandum. But in those dry-sounding texts were the seeds of two opposing revolutions in corporate America.

On August 10, 1971, two United Methodist ministers named Jack Corbett and Luther Tyson printed their "red herring"— their first prospectus for a new kind of mutual fund. The red herring takes its nickname from SEC-mandated red-ink warnings all over a prospectus's first page, cautioning investors about the risks they're taking. In this case, Tyson recalled, their red herring included "due warning that Pax World Management Corp. has had no previous experience in managing a fund. What a way to get started." [19]

Despite their complete lack of investment management experience, Corbett and Tyson were launching their fund because they had a novel vision that no professional money manager would touch: a socially responsible mutual fund. Pax World Funds was the first mutual fund to judge companies not only by their financial prospects but also by their compliance with several social screens. Did the companies make money from the Vietnam War? Did they have fair employment policies? Were they environmentally responsible?

The conventional wisdom in the investment world was that

picking a portfolio based on social responsibility was a surefire way to lose money. It was all very well for religious investors to avoid "sin stocks" like tobacco, alcohol, and gambling. That sort of thing had been going on for centuries. But to extend that principle and create an institution that systematically excluded socially irresponsible companies, rewarded ethical ones, and transformed borderline cases—that was utopian stuff, bad for business.

Corbett and Tyson had spent a year or two modeling their portfolio, and they were sure the conventional wisdom was wrong. But they couldn't find any fund managers who would join their risky experiment in ethical investing, so they turned to a handful of acquaintances with expertise in economics, business, and securities law. Together, they launched Pax World Funds.

Meanwhile, in one of those great historical coincidences, in Richmond, Virginia, a corporate lawyer and future Supreme Court justice named Lewis Powell was writing a very different manifesto for American business. His 6,000-word memorandum "Attack on American Free Enterprise System" was circulated secretly on August 23 by the U.S. Chamber of Commerce. Like Corbett and Tyson, Powell was stirred to action by some of the changes of 1960s America—student alienation and radicalism; widespread dissatisfaction with big corporations; and the rise of the modern equal rights, environmentalist, and consumer advocacy movements. But whereas the founders of Pax tried to reform American business in response to these new pressures, Powell called for business to mobilize and fight back on the battlefield of American politics: "Business must learn the lesson, long ago learned by labor and other self-interest groups. This is the lesson that political power is necessary; that such power must be assiduously cultivated; and that when necessary, it must be used aggressively and with determination—without embarrassment and without the reluctance which has been so characteristic of American business."[20]

Usually an understated, moderate man, Powell couched his distress call in the fervid language of life-and-death struggle: "Business and the enterprise system are in deep trouble, and the hour is late." The deadliest threat to capitalism, he argued, came not from communists but from the proliferating critics in respectable American institutions: college professors, journalists, intellectuals, lawyers, and politicians. Powell's response, in a nutshell, was "Look at the other side—at Ralph Nader, at the ACLU, at organized labor. We can do everything they're doing, in the media, the courts, and politics. But American business has the resources to do it bigger and better."

Powell's solution was relentlessly tactical. Step by step, he told the U.S. Chamber of Commerce how to turn the tables on the dangerous detractors of American corporations. He proposed new institutions, such as a "faculty of scholars" who would propagate business-friendly opinions and a "staff of lawyers" who would attempt to shift American law through carefully chosen court cases. He advocated "constant surveillance" of textbooks and television for an anticorporate slant. He demanded equal time for conservative speakers in both universities and the media and called on the Chamber to fund conservative mass-market books and television programming. Above all, Powell called on businessmen to engage boldly in politics, without any "reluctance to penalize politically" candidates whose views were unsympathetic to business. The whole project would be expensive, requiring "the scale of financing available only through joint effort."

Powell was himself a Democrat and a moderate on many social

issues (including abortion and affirmative action), but his vision for corporate America sparked the thirty-year campaign that culminated in Republican control of every branch of government.

At first, the U.S. Chamber of Commerce didn't know quite what to do with his ambitious scheme. Remember, at that time it wasn't a partisan clearinghouse. Within two years, however, Powell's manifesto had directly instigated the creation of a new style of politically aggressive think tank (the Heritage Foundation) and a relentlessly antiregulation legal institute (the Pacific Legal Foundation).[21] Both would inspire many imitators and have a huge impact on American law and policy.

On a broader level, the Powell Memorandum marked the point at which business became politically aggressive for the first time since the Great Depression. It is impossible to weigh the extent to which Powell directly inspired that movement. Few business leaders openly cited his memorandum, but more and more began acting according to Powell's dictum: "In the final analysis, the payoff—short of revolution—is what government does."

For example, in 1973 the National Association of Manufacturers moved its headquarters from New York to Washington, explaining, "The thing that affects business most today is government. The interrelationship of business with business is no longer so important as the interrelationship of business with government."[22] At around the same time, the CEOs of America's biggest companies formed the elite Business Roundtable to lobby against regulation.

The lobbyist became the symbol of this new era of corporate political clout, as an unprecedented surge of corporate money poured into influencing Congress. In 1971, only 175 American companies had registered lobbyists in Washington. A decade later, that number had grown to 2,445.[23] Today there are nearly

3,500 registered lobbying organizations and over 41,000 individual lobbyists.[24]

Contradictory Revolutions

The most remarkable thing about the conservative-corporate machine envisioned by Lewis Powell and the socially responsible investment institutions pioneered by Corbett and Tyson is not that they both revolutionized Wall Street but that they did so *at the same time.* These groundbreaking, seemingly incompatible trends were born in the same month in 1971, grew steadily throughout the next two decades, and surged into prominence by the turn of the millennium.

Pax World Funds trounced the conventional wisdom, proving both popular and financially successful. A host of other socially responsible investment funds joined the market in the 1980s. Most employed similar social screens; some focused on shareholder advocacy, trying to transform irresponsible companies from within. Between 1995 and 2005, the amount of money in socially responsible investment vehicles rose from $639 billion to $2.29 trillion.[25] In 1995, there were 55 socially screened funds on the Pax model—a remarkable increase over a quarter century. Ten years later, there were 201.[26]

Meanwhile, a circle of conservative billionaire financiers jointly turned Powell's manifesto into reality. They built a robust financial infrastructure to support dozens of newly launched think tanks, legal institutes, and media outlets. They purchased respectability for outlandish dogmas from the fringe of the Republican Party: tax cutting was the solution to all economic problems, massive deficits were good fiscal policy, most federal government regulations were unconstitutional, and environ-

mentalism was "nonviolent terrorism." Conservative ideologues deftly used their newfound money and political clout to
co-opt the growing army of corporate lobbyists, culminating in
the K Street Project. Religious and cultural conservatives
(whose creed would have been alien to the socially moderate,
consistently prochoice Powell) piggybacked to power on this
corporate-funded political machine. Moderate Republicans and
responsible business voices were sidelined; the money was on
the side of the radicals.

Today, both revolutions can boast of success. Roughly one in
every ten dollars under professional management in the United
States goes into socially responsible investment. In the decade
since 1995, socially responsible mutual funds grew at approxi-
mately 30 percent per year—more than three times the growth
rate for the U.S. investment industry as a whole. Pax World
Funds currently has $1.6 billion in assets under management,
and other progressive fund families such as Calvert Group and
Domini Social Investments are even larger.[27]

At the same time, as we have seen, most companies in the
S&P 500 now support the Republican Party, which has successfully leveraged business dollars to expand its control. A tidal
wave of corporate money has backed the steady advance of
right-wing ideologues through both houses of Congress, the
White House, and the Supreme Court. The ultimate result, for
the long years under George W. Bush, was a government that
was neither socially nor environmentally responsible.

How could two contradictory revolutions succeed in corporate America at the same time? Sadly, there has been a crucial
failure of vision in the "corporate social responsibility" revolution. Progressive investors have turned a blind eye to the collaboration between conservative politics and big business despite

its negative effects. As a result, socially responsible investment today is in danger of becoming a "red herring" in the worst sense—a misleading distraction from a critical problem.

Beyond the Red Herring

This isn't to say that socially responsible investment isn't a good idea. It's a great idea—one that needs to be applied to a much wider range of corporate behavior. Just as Corbett and Tyson realized that they couldn't limit their vision to screening out "sin stocks," today we have to look beyond the obvious social and environmental impacts and judge companies on their *political* impact as well.

If progressive funds applied the same screen to the Republican Party that they applied to the companies in their portfolio, that party would never pass muster. Imagine judging the George W. Bush administration on categories such as environmental sustainability, fair labor practices, consumer protection, and community impact. Yet these funds, and their mostly unsuspecting investors, continue to support companies that pour money into the Republican Party.

Joseph F. Keefe, current president and CEO of Pax World Management Corp. (the investment advisory company behind Pax World Funds), issued a paper in fall 2006 that forcefully challenged this blind spot of the socially responsible investment world: "To talk about investing in sustainability, when the same companies the SRI industry congratulates for publishing sustainability reports are engaged in political efforts—through their lobbying, PAC and soft-money contributions—to weaken environmental standards, is to perpetuate a disconnect that undermines the effectiveness of SRI."[28] He went on to argue that SRI funds need to understand that their real constituency is a political one: blue investors, who "would like to see their investment decisions as well as their voting patterns help advance a progressive agenda."

Many socially responsible investors, especially big institutions, might respond that they have a duty to be politically neutral in their investment decisions. For some, that's true. But if 77 percent of the top companies in your portfolio are donating heavily to the Republican Party, *your investment dollars are already partisan.* Being politically neutral is not the same as being politically blind. A truly neutral portfolio would have a rough balance between companies that donate to Republicans and companies that donate to Democrats, instead of just accepting the bias of the S&P 500.

In the end, many progressive investors aren't really afraid of being partisan with their investment dollars. They're afraid of losing money by screening out financially successful but politically irresponsible companies. It's a reheated version of the same conventional wisdom that forced Corbett and Tyson to launch their own fund back in 1971. Too many people still buy into the idea that responsible companies are likely to be financially unsuccessful.

The relative success of socially responsible investment should have debunked this myth long ago. Socially screened portfolios have on the whole generated returns similar to major indexes, and some have done a bit better. In 2004, the management consultancy McKinsey & Company found that over ten years, a socially responsible investment portfolio had "generated returns of 8 to 14 percent . . . [which is] comparable to capital market returns."[29] An academic study in 2003 analyzed the results of fifty-two previous studies of corporate social responsibility and found a positive relationship between a company's social performance and its financial performance.[30] Other studies claim to have found a positive link between greater responsibility and higher profits, most promisingly in the area of ecoefficiency.[31] Being socially responsible clearly does not cripple companies.

But neither does it seem to give them a huge advantage—at least not in the ways in which the big progressive funds have measured "social responsibility." Of the biggest ten large-cap SRI mutual funds, only three outperformed the S&P 500 over the last five years.[32] The latest research by Professor David Vogel of the Haas School of Business (in his critically praised book *The Market for Virtue)* suggests that social responsibility is a neutral factor.[33] On the whole, it is not a strong predictor of which companies will fail and which will outperform the market.

What about being politically responsible? Until the November 2006 elections, Republicans dominated every branch of American government for six years, and you would expect companies that "back the winner" to be more successful. We've all seen headlines about big oil companies and government contractors gaining special benefits from being close to the center of power. Political contributions are supposedly all about getting access—and what good is it for a company to have access to a party that doesn't control any branch of government? Wouldn't investors be shooting themselves in the foot by limiting themselves to the few companies that favor the Democrats?

Like Corbett and Tyson, we put the conventional wisdom to the test by modeling a politically responsible portfolio. We created a "Blue Index" of all the companies in the S&P 500 index that were socially responsible *and* had supported the Democrats over the last five election cycles. We had expected these companies to be successful, but the extent of their success surprised even us.

If you had invested $100 in the 500 current constituents of

Stock market performance of blue companies compared to red companies and the S&P 500

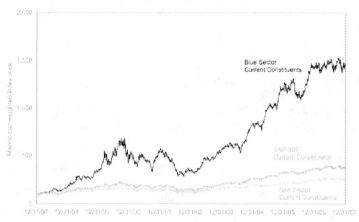

the S&P 500 on December 31, 2002, after five years you would have had $256—a decent enough return. On the other hand, if you had put the same amount into the 76 current constituents of the Blue Index, your investment would have more than quadrupled to $428. A $100 investment in the 380 "red" companies would have yielded only $204, below the market rate of return. Over the past five years, the Blue Index has outperformed the market by 13.07 percent annually and has outperformed red S&P 500 companies by 18.42 percent.[34]

If we look at their ten-year record, the numbers are even more striking. Your $100 investment in the current constituents of the Blue Index from 1997 onward would have grown over tenfold, to a whopping $1,435—compared to $377 for the current constituents of the S&P 500 and $262 for the current red companies over the same period.

The Blue Sector's record speaks for itself. Progressive

investors do not need to choose between making money and making a difference, both socially and politically. Being blue puts companies in the black.

Completing the Revolution

The success of the Blue Sector undermines some of the most widespread fictions about business and politics in America: that there is an inevitable trade-off between conscience and profit; that hardheaded, right-wing policies are best for big business; or that progressives are bleeding hearts who don't know how to make money.

The simple truth is that there is no good reason for Republicans to dominate corporate America as they do. Rather, the preponderance of "red" companies is another sign that too many CEOs have been mesmerized by the siren call of short-term advantage—a tune the Republicans have been happy to sing as they cut taxes, gut regulatory agencies, and promote wasteful consumption of energy and resources. Some businesses and corporate barons certainly benefit from these policies in the short term. Overall, though, most Americans (including most businesses) and the economy as a whole suffer when the government is feeble or pursues irresponsible, unsustainable policies.

Lewis Powell and the millionaires who followed his blueprint were convinced that their political machine was necessary to save capitalism. Ironically, the abuses of that machine have done more to damage the credibility of corporate America than to save it. As discussed in the last chapter, the short-term vision of Republican companies and politicians produced burdensome financial policing and a plunge in corporate America's public reputation—a 2006 World Economic Forum Survey showed a 19 percent drop in Americans who "trusted" corporations over the previous two years.[35] In 2006, Americans overwhelmingly voted to restore balance to our country's politics. It's past time to restore balance to American business as well.

The first step is to complete the socially responsible investment revolution begun by Corbett and Tyson. Conscientious investors and funds should begin screening out politically irresponsible companies as well as environmental and social offenders. By investing in the Blue Sector, investors can support a progressive agenda and beat the market at the same time. Similarly, by favoring blue companies in their shopping decisions, progressive consumers not only make a small positive political impact but also ultimately do themselves a favor. We all gain when an economically responsible government is in power. We all gain from a model of business that respects the environment and employees' well-being.

In our next chapter, we look at the Blue Sector in more detail. What kind of companies pass the blue test? Why have they been so successful? By examining the traits that thriving blue companies have in common, we can identify principles to help revive progressive politics as a whole.

CHAPTER 3

Being Blue Puts Companies in the Black

ACCORDING TO THE CONTEMPORARY, CONSERVATIVE Republican model of business, all the good behavior that goes by the name of "corporate social responsibility" is just a distraction from a company's primary mission: earning a profit. Corporations shouldn't worry about broader issues such as water pollution, health care for their workforce, or the social and economic conditions in the communities where they make their money. The conservative Republicans talk about American business as though it were fragile: if we burden it with too much accountability or too many expectations, it will wither.

Of course, corporate profits as a share of national wealth have never been higher—and this surge in profit began under a Democratic president who believed in corporate responsibility and constructive government regulation of the economy.[1] Corporate prosperity hasn't depended on Republican efforts to remove all controls on business. Still, the conservative model insists that the only responsibility of business is not to break the law. Meanwhile, Republicans are busily revising the law to take out any provision that constrains or regulates business.

For example, one of George W. Bush's first acts in office was to throw out the ergonomics and workplace safety requirements mandated by the Clinton administration.[2] Then, in 2003, the Bush administration fought successfully in Congress to curtail companies' obligation to pay overtime, affecting up to 8 million workers.[3] In 2005, the Republican-led Congress "reformed" consumer bankruptcy law at the expense of middle- and low-income debtors—many of whom are prey to unethical marketing, extortionate interest rates, and lax identity theft protection by banks and credit card companies.[4] The Republican government has consistently acted on the principle that the cost of corporate decisions should fall on everyday citizens, not on corporations.

Where Republicans can't rewrite the law, they ignore it, as the Bush EPA attempted with the Clean Air Act. The law states that "any physical change" to an old coal plant must be accompanied by modern pollution control measures. In 2003, the EPA tried to slip in a qualifier that this really meant any *major* physical change—that is, change costing more than 20 percent of the value of the plant—a standard that would have allowed old coal plants to expand dramatically without getting any cleaner. The D.C. Court of Appeals made short work of this obfuscation, commenting dryly that the EPA had shown "no reason why 'any' should not mean 'any.'"[5]

Behind the relentless Republican drive for deregulation lies a profoundly mistaken idea: that corporate spending is a zero-sum game. According to this misconception, every dollar a company invests in worker benefits, community development, or the environment is one less dollar invested in profit-making activities. If that were true, a socially responsible company would be choosing principle over profits and would lose out to other companies that keep their focus on the financial bottom line.

> **Myth: Socially responsible companies are bound to underperform the market.**

Whether true or not, this conservative dogma is out of touch with the thinking of a majority of business leaders. In a 2003 global survey by PricewaterhouseCoopers, 68 percent of CEOs expressed the view that "the proper exercise of corporate social responsibility is linked to profitability."[6] A steadily growing number of business schools now require a course in corporate social responsibility: 54 percent in 2006, up from 45 percent in 2003 and 34 percent in 2001, according to the Aspen Institute.[7] These schools and executives recognize that any company that hopes to be around for more than a few years must have an interest in the long-term well-being of its employees, its community, and the environment. They also recognize the abiding damage to a company's reputation and brand that can ensue from legal but irresponsible behavior. A responsible company may face higher costs today, but that money is an investment in the health of its business tomorrow.

Of course, as the oil companies show, in the short term there's plenty of money to be made by unsustainable exploitation of labor and natural resources. Exxon Mobil, the poster child for corporate irresponsibility, reported the highest annual profits of any company in history: $39.5 billion for fiscal year 2006.[8] (The previous record holder? Exxon Mobil, with profits of $36.1 billion in 2005.) In a pinch, plenty of companies manage to stay profitable through socially and environmentally irresponsible strategies instead of through innovation and investment in their workforce. We shouldn't be surprised that some of the most profitable American corporations are big polluters or union bashers. But a vibrant minority of progressive companies in nearly every economic sector manages to outperform the market while still meeting the criteria of corporate social responsibility.

We believe that the roots of this achievement go deeper than mere compliance with a set of rules. The success of Blue Sector companies stems from visionary leadership and a progressive corporate culture—a deeply felt, companywide commitment to ethical, sustainable growth. Mainstream indices of corporate social responsibility don't necessarily capture a company's values on this level. For example, a corporation may meet environmental standards by happenstance, to generate friendly publicity, or to keep activists off its back. There's no reason to expect any of those traits to correlate strongly with success. Some companies, on the other hand, embrace ecoefficiency because they're planning to be around for the long term and have thought seriously about what that implies.

We propose a simple litmus test to separate the companies with a long-term vision from those that are simply bending with the winds of public opinion. Do they put their political money where their mouth is? In the sad state of affairs where one American party has made itself a standard-bearer for short-term, unsustainable, irresponsible corporate behavior, where does a company choose to invest its political capital? The results of our test prove that companies don't have to choose between being progressive and being profitable.

> **Reality: "Blue" companies, which are both socially and politically responsible, are beating the market in virtually every sector of the American economy.**

Exactly what kind of companies do we find in the Blue Sector? When we put together the Blue Index, we applied a double test to every company in the S&P 500: a company had to "give blue" as well as "act blue."

"Give Blue"

Our research team monitors all political contributions by senior executives affiliated with S&P 500 companies and by S&P 500 companies to political action commities, selecting only those companies that gave at least 50 percent of their political contributions to Democratic candidates over the last four election cycles.

"Act Blue"

- Environmental sustainability
- Responsible corporate governance
- Respect for human rights at home and abroad
- Diversity in the workforce and in leadership
- Fair treatment of all employees
- Avoidance of products that cause great social harm

Our criteria are simple but powerful. When we say that a company "gives blue," we mean that over the last decade that company has sent at least 50 percent of its political contributions to Democratic candidates. When we say that a company "acts blue," we mean that its business practices respect core progressive values.

In gauging whether a company gives blue, we measure all

the donations from a company's political action committee (PAC) and political contributions from its top three executives over the current and previous four election cycles. A company with a strong red record can't turn blue overnight by making one big donation to a particular Democrat.

Our measurement of giving blue doesn't favor big corporate donors over small donors; as long as the company gives most of its political dollars to Democrats, we count it as blue, regardless of the scale of its contributions. We want to gauge the progressive attitudes of the executives, not the importance of politics to their industry. In general, the Blue Index isn't designed to increase the flow of money into politics. We see investing in the Blue Sector as a step toward rebalancing the system, stemming the flood of money to the Republicans, and encouraging companies to reconsider the political consequences of their contributions.

In fact, plenty of blue companies give sparingly. Most of them are blue on the strength of their executive donations, not PAC contributions. This sets them apart strikingly from the rest of the S&P 500. Of the $316 million contributed to politics by S&P 500 companies over the last five election cycles, $285 million (roughly 90 percent) came from corporate PACs. In all, 310 companies in the index, or 62 percent, have PACs. By contrast, only 24 of the 76 blue companies (32 percent) have a PAC.[9] There's nothing wrong with having a PAC if it adds shareholder value, but on the evidence, blue companies and their executives tend to be more disciplined when it comes to spending company money on politics.

Acting blue is just as important as giving blue. We screen all the Blue Index companies against nine fundamental social responsibility benchmarks. We don't want to recommend investing in companies with poor corporate governance, unfair labor policies, damaging environmental practices, or disregard for human rights in America and abroad. Nor will we include companies that profit from socially harmful products like tobacco and firearms. Each of our nine screens is detailed and requires in-depth monitoring of corporate behavior. On the environmental front, among other things, we look at a company's carbon footprint, check its record for violations of federal air and water regulations, and consider its hazardous waste production. For our corporate governance screen, we weigh the company's transparency and accountability and take a critical look at its CEO and board compensation policy; we also give black marks for recent accounting scandals or associations with other ethically troubled firms.

To make sure we catch any company that stops acting blue, we work with an independent research firm, KLD Research & Analytics. KLD sends us weekly updates on whether the companies in the Blue Index are still behaving in a way that is consistent with progressive values. Wherever KLD expresses a "concern," we count it as a strike against the company. If a company gets three strikes—that is, if it clearly ceases to be socially and environmentally responsible—we drop it from the index, regardless of how much money it donates to the Democrats.

We haven't had to drop very many companies, though. Of the 80 S&P 500 corporations that donate mostly to Democrats, 76 pass our social responsibility screen. The failure rate of the remaining 420 red and neutral companies in the index is more than twice as high.[10] Not surprisingly, the data suggest that progressive politics correlate with progressive social values.

The blue companies include some of America's most innovative and thriving companies across a wide range of industries.

Blue Sector Companies Include

Apple	Starbucks Corporation
The Gap	Nike
Whole Foods Market	Starwood Hotels & Resorts Worldwide
Google	E*Trade Financial
Simon Property Group	Estée Lauder
KeySpan Corporation	Harman International Industries
Liz Claiborne	State Street Corporation
Vornado Realty Trust	Bank of New York
Lehman Brothers	Sempra Energy
Mattel	Progressive Corporation

Plenty of blue companies are household names, and even the less famous ones are disproportionately likely to crop up in the business press. For example, since 1997 *BusinessWeek* has published an annual ranking of the top 50 performers in the S&P 500. Four times in the last five years, the best-performing company in America has been blue; Forest Labs took the number one spot in 2003, Progressive in 2004, Apple in 2006, and Google in 2007. That's an 80 percent record in the top slot, even though the Blue Sector makes up only 16 percent of the S&P 500. In fact, in 2007, blue companies not only held the number one and number two spots (Google and Coach), they held twelve of the top 40 spots on *BusinessWeek*'s list. More than a dozen blue companies have been regulars on the list of top performers over the years, including Nike, Qualcomm, Adobe, Fannie Mae, Starbucks, and Electronic Arts.[11]

We weren't surprised that progressive companies outperformed the market; we already knew that progressive politicians were better managers of the American economy, so why wouldn't progressive business leaders also be better at running companies? Still, to be sure we hadn't missed anything that might explain away the Blue Sector, we had our data checked by an independent research firm, Competition Policy Associates, which reviewed the information and validated our results. At that point, we began bringing our index to the attention of a skeptical investment world.

Believe It or Not

When we tell investors companies that donate to Democrats tend to be more successful than the rest of the market, the most common initial response is disbelief. Despite the success enjoyed by many socially responsible indexes and companies, people are reluctant to let go of the myth that acting blue—let alone giving blue—is a sign that a company puts politics ahead of profits.

Many have asked if the success of the Blue Sector is somehow a coincidence. We ran the data through a barrage of statistical tests to rule out pure chance. For example, using what's known as the "Monte Carlo" method, we used computer modeling to randomly generate 10 million market-capitalization-weighted portfolios of 76 companies currently in the S&P 500. If the performance of the Blue Index were the result of chance, you'd expect a significant number of randomly generated portfolios to beat the Blue Index. Instead, the Blue Index outperformed 99.8 percent of the computer-generated portfolios.

Some critics who saw just the graph of Blue Index performance versus S&P 500 performance suggested that we had been taken in by "survivorship bias," a relatively common mistake that people make when they compare a portfolio of today's stocks to yesterday's market. If you look at the five-year performance of any group of existing stocks with some random factor in common—say, of all the companies that have the color blue in their corporate logos—they'll often outperform the S&P 500 index over the same period, because the market index includes all the companies that failed and went bankrupt over those five years. The blue-logo companies share more than a color on their letterhead in common; they have the easily overlooked but major advantage that they survived this five-year period. Fortunately, whenever we run our performance comparisons, we compare the current Blue Index companies to the 500 *current constituents* of the S&P 500, not to the S&P 500 of five years ago. All the companies have survived to the present. Some have done much better than others.

Of course, many factors contribute to a company's success. How can we be sure that the "Blue Factor" (the combination of giving blue and acting blue) is really so significant? We compared the predictive power of the Blue Factor with that of a familiar financial metric: the P/E (price-earnings) ratio, the measure of a company's share price relative to its earnings. The P/E ratio can be calculated using either forecasted earnings (a "forward P/E") or reported past earnings (a "trailing P/E"). We compared both metrics to the Blue Factor, using an analysis in which a low p value (probability) indicates a good predictive tool. Our results confirmed that over the last five years the Blue Factor ($p = 0.0021$) was a better predictor of a given stock's likelihood of outperforming the market than either a low forward ($p = 0.0779$) or trailing ($p = 0.0205$) P/E ratio.[12]

Some suggest that the success of the Blue Index is an optical illusion, that we're just measuring the success of a bunch of high-tech companies that have had a good few years. In fact, blue companies consistently do better across eleven out of twelve

Market-Cap-Weighted Average Share Price Growth of Blue Companies Compared to the Performance of Their Sectors over the Last 5 Years[13]

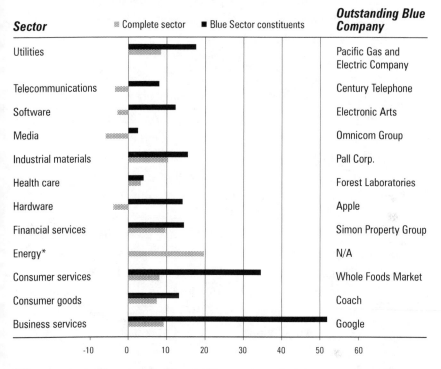

Sector	Complete sector / Blue Sector constituents	*Outstanding Blue Company*
Utilities		Pacific Gas and Electric Company
Telecommunications		Century Telephone
Software		Electronic Arts
Media		Omnicom Group
Industrial materials		Pall Corp.
Health care		Forest Laboratories
Hardware		Apple
Financial services		Simon Property Group
Energy*		N/A
Consumer services		Whole Foods Market
Consumer goods		Coach
Business services		Google

* No companies in this sector currently meet blue company criteria.

sectors of the economy. Blue consumer goods companies outperform the consumer goods sector as a whole, and so on, as this graph shows.

Thus it can't be the case that blue companies succeed only because they tend to be found in less regulated industries, industries with high volatility, or industries with strong overall growth trends. Blue companies outperform the competition in every sector of the economy where they exist. The top three "Most Admired Real Estate Companies" are part of the Blue Index,[14] as are some of America's most successful utilities (such as PG&E and Sempra Energy). Even in sectors that have had a rough five years, with overall negative performance—media, software, hardware, telecommunications—the blue companies in that sector have collectively stayed profitable.

To turn the tables for a moment, just imagine how poorly the red companies would be doing if the energy sector (mainly oil and gas extraction firms) hadn't been booming. At the moment, no energy company meets Blue Index criteria—all of them fail either the environmental test or the political contribution test (generally both). As the earlier graph shows, the energy sector has generated markedly stronger returns than any other sector over the last five years. High oil prices have been a windfall for energy companies, as well as for Republicans, who receive more than 80 percent of oil and gas company contributions.[15] Yet even without a single company from this lucrative sector, the Blue Sector handily outperforms the market as a whole.

Nor is the power of a progressive business model limited to large companies. We ran a similar comparison with the Russell 2000 Index of small-cap companies, and over the past five years the 371 blue companies in the Russell outperformed the 2,000 current constituents of the index, albeit by a smaller margin.

Some people might still suspect that at the end of the day, the performance of the Blue Sector is driven by a handful of hugely successful companies that just happen to be blue. In fact, even if we removed all blue companies with market capitalizations in excess of $25 billion—including Apple, Google, and Starbucks—the remaining Blue Index companies would still have outperformed the current S&P 500 by approximately 3 percent per year.[16] Three percent may not sound like a lot, but when you're talking about stocks, beating the market by 3 percent is great—better than the vast majority of investment strategies. The Blue Sector outclasses the competition even with its strongest arm tied behind its back.

Of course, not every individual blue company is a success story. We aren't just cherry-picking the most successful progressive firms. The companies in the Blue Index aren't the top 76 blue companies in the S&P 500—they're the *only* 76 blue companies in the S&P 500. Some of them lose money. But, taken collectively, they've beaten the market by an impressive margin.

Explaining the Blue Factor

We were the first to spot this trend, but we haven't been the only ones. Several months after we designed the Blue Index, three business school professors, Michael Cooper, Huseyin Gulen, and Alexei Ovtchinnikov, published a paper entitled "Corporate Political Contributions and Stock Returns."[17] These three scholars had analyzed all political contributions by corporate PACs to congressional races between 1979 and 2004. They found a clearly positive "contribution effect" on the stock prices of the contributing companies. Corporations that gave PAC money to many House and Senate candidates over a given five-year period tended to enjoy higher stock prices during the following twelve years, especially relative to corporations that didn't contribute.

Who benefits most from the contribution effect? Cooper, Gulen, and Ovtchinnikov confirmed that over the last quarter century, Republicans have tended to receive more corporate money and be supported by a greater number of companies than

Democrats. On the three scholars' reckoning, the average American company supports 61 percent Republican candidates and 39 percent Democrats. Given the clear preference of corporate donors for the GOP, the authors note, "one might hypothesize that the contribution effect should be greater for Republican contributing firms."[18] Yet in fact the authors found that contributions to Democrats were linked to a markedly greater jump in stock price than were contributions to GOP candidates.

Cooper, Gulen, and Ovtchinnikov were reluctant to speculate on exactly why this might be the case—or indeed, why the contribution effect exists at all. That wasn't the focus of their study. They did suggest a few different ways in which politicians can directly benefit firms: "favorable tax treatment and or credits, the awarding of government contracts, the imposing of tariffs or other penalties on competitors, and implementing favorable regulatory requirements."[19] Other analysts, looking over their results, suggested that Democrats are usually the "swing voters" on business-related legislation and that for any firm "trying to assemble a critical mass of votes, that marginal Democratic vote is worth a lot."[20]

The academics are right, of course—there are countless cases of companies earning huge benefits from their political contributions. One recent example foisted on the American taxpayer is the Research Partnership to Secure Energy for America (RPSEA), an alliance of seventeen publicly traded energy companies such as Chevron and Halliburton.[21] In 2005, RPSEA successfully lobbied the U.S. government to fund its ten-year, $400 million research project into "ultra-deepwater" drilling for oil and gas. The RPSEA member companies made $100 billion in profits in 2005 alone, but instead of committing $40 million a year as a long-term investment in this research, they invested far smaller amounts in politics over the 2000 and 2004 election cycles: $171,498 to Representative Joe Barton (R.-Tex.), $91,300 to House Majority Leader Tom DeLay, and smaller amounts to other Republican and Democratic legislators. Not surprisingly, their $400 million project was slipped into the 2005 energy bill early on the morning of the vote, after the supposedly "final" version of the bill had been drafted. The RPSEA investment in politicians on both sides of the aisle (totaling about $350,000) was repaid more than a thousandfold by that single clause. This sort of thing surely explains much of the "contribution effect" identified by Cooper, Gulen, and Ovtchinnikov.

Pork-barrel politics cannot explain the dramatic success of the Blue Sector over the last five to ten years. After the Republican takeover of Congress in 1994, Democrats became less and less able to offer concrete legislative benefits of any kind; for much of the last decade, they were thoroughly shut out of power. As for the "swing voter" argument, the recently ousted GOP Congress was notorious for its practice of locking out the minority party, resolving differences internally, and passing bills on the strength of Republican votes alone.[22] If a piece of legislation looked as if it would require Democratic swing votes to pass, Dennis Hastert and Tom DeLay would usually withdraw it or not introduce it in the first place. The blue companies that contribute to the Democrats have been thriving despite the fact that the Democrats really haven't been able to offer them much.

The real reason for the Blue Sector's success, we are convinced, lies in the leadership and corporate culture of the blue companies themselves, not in any direct benefit the companies may derive from their political spending. Business leaders who tend to donate to the Democrats are more likely to buy into progressive values, and progressive values are positively linked to business success. That's the real story of the Blue Sector—a story about the power of progressive leadership.

The link between progressive values and business success has gone unnoticed largely thanks to the common practice that we call "bluewashing." Most progressive activists will be familiar with the concept of a "greenwash," in which a big corporate polluter adopts a handful of superficially ecofriendly policies, usually trumpeted by a pricey advertising campaign, while furtively continuing to pollute and lobby for less stringent pollution controls. Similarly, a bluewashed company looks more socially responsible than it really is. Bluewashers see corporate social responsibility as a matter for the public relations department and do the minimum necessary to satisfy critics, advocacy groups, and social screens.

These companies are making a crucial mistake. Our research suggests that companies are more likely to succeed when they go beyond the minimum and genuinely internalize progressive, socially responsible principles. Short of a polygraph test, the best indicator we currently have of this internalization is a company's political contributions. By no coincidence, Blue Sector companies tend to excel in certain areas (such as innovation, flexibility, and ecoefficiency) that also reflect key advantages of progressive politics over conservative politics. We call these interlinked principles the Six Pillars of Progressive Leadership and we'll explain them in the next two chapters. Blue companies don't simply talk about these principles. They act on them and live by them.

CHAPTER 4

The Principles of Progressive Leadership I

Innovation, Flexibility, Ecoefficiency

THE STRONG PERFORMANCE OF BLUE COMPANIES is a shock to conservative ideologues who think that progressive economic principles are essentially watered-down communism. The Blue Sector equally challenges the assumptions of investors who consider political contributions to be an ordinary business expense that is unrelated to partisan allegiance or corporate culture.

Some industries need access to government, these politically neutral investors would argue, especially in heavily regulated sectors such as banking, aviation, and telecoms. It's no surprise to find companies from those industries making large investments in political parties and candidates—and no surprise that those investments would tend to favor the incumbent party. Surely the balance of power in Washington sufficiently explains the Republican slant of the last few years. These investors argue that a few companies may favor the Republicans for ideological reasons, but for the most part, they were just paying for access during a time when the GOP held a virtual monopoly on government.

In this view, the important question about political contributions is not whether they are going to a progressive or a conservative party so much as whether they are going to a party with the power to get things done in Washington. This vision of business dismisses the argument that a company's progressive political contributions are part of a broader pattern of progressive leadership.

> **Myth: Political donations are just "pay-to-play" payments to the party in power and don't reflect anything deeper about a company.**

We recognize that companies make political contributions for plenty of reasons other than partisan leanings. Access is one essential reason. We would expect the party in power to enjoy a fund-raising advantage, and we would expect to see higher levels of political spending by companies in highly regulated industries.

The corporate slant toward Republicans, however, goes beyond what access alone can explain. It doesn't just reflect a preference for the party in power; the slant existed before George W. Bush, before the 1994 Republican takeover of Congress. Most big corporations contribute to Republicans because they want to and to Democrats when they have to. The unfortunate truth is that over the decades since the Powell Memorandum, corporate America has by and large come to accept the flawed conservative vision of business and politics. The relative underperformance of red companies suggests that investors are unwittingly suffering for their mistake.

The success of the Blue Sector, however, defies any theory of political contributions that focuses exclusively on access to power. For the past ten years, the best-performing companies have been net donors to a party with steadily *declining* political clout. From 2002 to 2006, the Democrats were helpless on Capitol Hill and shut out of the White House, but blue companies continued to thrive. If access is the explanation for political donations, how can contributions to the party in opposition be one of the best indicators of corporate success?

Contributions to parties and candidates represent a small proportion of most corporations' total spending. In microcosm, however, they reflect vital aspects of a company's culture—and of the leadership that has shaped that culture. Companies whose executives share the Republican Party's penchant for short-term benefits and unsustainable business practices tend to contribute disproportionately to the GOP; companies whose executives take a broader, more sustainable vision of corporate interest tend to contribute to the Democrats. In our observations, these blue companies tend to be innovative, flexible, and environmentally aware; they tend to treat their employees fairly and respond constructively to critics. In other words, they tend to display Six Pillars of Progressive Leadership:

A culture of innovation	Investment in employees' well-being
Organizational flexibility	Constructive relationships with critics
Ecoefficiency	Long-term perspective

Not all blue companies share these traits, of course, and not all red companies lack them. We aren't claiming that every CEO who consistently donates to the Democratic Party is automatically transformed into a brilliant innovator and visionary who works hand in glove with labor unions and Greenpeace while simultaneously receiving *BusinessWeek*'s highest plaudits. Some blue companies are more consistently progressive than others, and some are dramatically more successful. In an environment as complex as the U.S. economy, we wouldn't expect any single cause to explain everything or any single factor to correlate perfectly with financial success.

What we're describing are broad positive tendencies, more common among blue companies than in corporate America as a whole. Because these positive traits correlate with demonstrable market success, we think that, taken collectively, they offer the best explanation for the undeniable fact of Blue Sector outperformance. In this chapter and the next, we lay out facts and stories that illustrate the six pillars in practice.

> **Reality: Blue companies not only tend to have greater financial success but also tend to be more innovative, flexible, and ecoefficient than other companies.**

Pillar I: A Culture of Innovation

Everyone recognizes the importance of innovation for success in today's economy. Most of America's top corporate winners are innovators—whether they've capitalized on a newly invented technology or revolutionized an established industry with a fresh approach to logistics, organization, or marketing.

Like success itself, however, innovation is more easily perceived than achieved. For investors, the challenge is how to recognize promising ideas and get behind them early on. For companies, the challenge is figuring out what exactly they can do to foster innovation. Plowing money into research alone won't do it; as *BusinessWeek* pointed out in a late-2006 review of global innovation, "The company with the biggest R&D budget in 2005 was Ford Motor. Eight billion dollars later . . . the company is hardly a paragon of innovation."[1] (Ford Motor Company, by the way, is as garishly red as the Ford Torino in *Starsky & Hutch,* with 78 percent of its $2 million in corporate contributions over the past decade going to the Republicans).[2]

Rather, the key to benefiting from innovation seems to be a particular kind of corporate culture. Companies need to create it, investors need to recognize it. It's the kind of culture that embraces change, opens up communication, fosters experimentation, breaks rules, and rewards creativity. It is, in a word, progressive. Innovation flourishes alongside progressive habits of mind, such as open-mindedness, acceptance of diversity, and the conviction that big problems (whether of society or business) should be solved rather than dodged.

We don't think it's a coincidence that America's last Democratic administration presided over a historic boom in innovation. Progressive government is better suited to foster a national culture of innovation, thanks in part to its openness and optimism and in part to the Democratic embrace of policies such as:

- Restraining would-be monopolists from crushing small, creative upstarts
- Shoring up the social safety net that makes it possible for ordinary Americans to afford to take risks

- Funding the kinds of scientific research that Republicans avoid to appease their fundamentalist base
- Paying down the government deficit in order to lower interest rates and boost private investment and small business

In a similar fashion, companies run by progressive leaders are more likely to achieve a culture of innovation. A disproportionate number of Blue Sector companies are creative leaders and noted innovators in their industries. In *Fortune* magazine's 2006 ranking of the "Most Admired Companies," 40 percent of the companies most admired for their innovations are blue, even though the Blue Sector represents only 16 percent of the S&P 500.[3] A recent global innovation report by the consultancy Booz Allen Hamilton identified the blue companies Apple, Fisher Scientific, Forest Labs, Google, and SanDisk as exemplary "high-leverage innovators"—companies that get an exceptionally high return on their research spending.[4]

As an example, consider one of the best-known Blue Sector companies, Apple—a company whose executives have given more than 95 percent of their political contributions to Democrats over the last decade and whose stock price has outpaced the S&P 500 by 34.0 percent over the past ten years. Since Steve Jobs took the reins as CEO in 1997, Apple has embodied innovation in the computer and electronics industries. Its most recent and famous successes are the iPod, an icon of cutting-edge technology and design, the market-expanding iTunes digital music delivery service, and the recently introduced iPhone.

It's instructive to compare these breakthroughs with the attitude of rival company Dell toward Apple and its products. At the beginning of Steve Jobs' tenure, Michael S. Dell suggested that, were he in charge of Apple, "I'd shut it down and give the money back to the shareholders."[5] When pressed about the rise of Apple's iPod player by a *BusinessWeek* reporter in 2004, an exasperated Dell executive replied, "It's a fine product, but why would we want to focus [much energy] on that little stuff. It's like being the King of MousePads!"[6] Recently, Apple's market capitalization surpassed that of Dell, a company that gives more than 90 percent of its political contributions to Republicans. The contrast between Dell and Apple illustrates a key principle of progressive business: when faced with a major challenge, progressive companies don't simply grab at easy cost-cutting measures but invest in their strengths and search for new, nonobvious ways to advance.

The inventiveness and creative thinking of blue companies aren't limited to technology-driven industries but exists across all sectors of the economy, from grocery retailing to real estate to insurance. The innovative companies in these industries chose not to follow the herd but rather were the first in their sector to harness a new technology, adopt a new business model, or target a previously untapped market.

For example, take Simon Property Group, "generally considered to be the [real estate] industry's most innovative organization."[7] Simon was the first retail real estate company that set out to create a brand for itself, not just for the stores that were housed in its malls. It aggressively pursued alternative income streams, including Simon Mall Gift Cards and advertising partnerships with nonretail companies. The company's ability to create and execute new strategies put it on track to become the largest publicly traded and most highly admired real estate investment trust in the country. In the past six election cycles, Simon Property Group's top three executives have donated more than $93,000 (84 percent of their total political giving) to Democratic candidates and causes. Over the last ten years, the company's stock has outperformed the S&P 500 by 14.4 percent.

Or consider Progressive, which has emerged as one of the most important players in the automotive insurance sector. It has led the way in applying new communications technology to its industry, like the TripSensor, a logging device that can plug into a car's engine computer and record mileage, speed, and other relevant driving behavior. Progressive also holds a patent on the use of vehicle monitoring systems (global positioning satellite devices and cell phones) for the same purpose. Customers who voluntarily sign up for these new tracking systems enjoy insurance premium discounts linked to their actual driving habits.[8]

Business analysts have also praised Progressive's "solid record of innovation in customer service." The company pioneered several "concierge-like services," such as letting customers rent a car at a Progressive store to drive while their vehicle is under repair.[9] It was also one of the first insurance companies to capitalize on the opportunities presented by the Internet, especially in the area of comparative price quotes. Progressive's executives have given more than 97 percent of their political contributions to Democrats over the last decade.

Innovative drugs are the lifeblood of the pharmaceutical industry, and most big pharmaceutical companies have enormous research and development budgets. The industry is dominated by behemoth red companies like Pfizer and Eli Lilly, both of which have given 73 to 74 percent of their political contributions to Republicans over the past decade. The blue company Forest Laboratories bucks the industry trend, both in its political contributions (it has no PAC, and its executives give 95 percent to Democrats) and in its approach to developing new drugs. The company's counterintuitive innovation was to spend *less* on its own original research. Instead, it finds promising new drugs researched by other companies—especially foreign ones that lack access to U.S. markets—and offers to handle the development, manufacturing, and marketing of those drugs in America. This division of labor may not sound like a groundbreaking advance, but it earned Forest Laboratories profits that the conventional, vertically integrated drug giants have been trying to emulate. Over the last ten years, Forest Laboratories' stock has outperformed the S&P 500 by 19.3 percent. Forest ranked number one among *BusinessWeek*'s 50 best-performing companies in 2003 and was one of the "high-leverage innovators" recognized by Booz Allen Hamilton's 2006 Global Innovators list.[10]

Blue company innovation is often closely linked to the second pillar of progressive leadership: a flat, flexible organization structure that encourages and rewards creative thinking.

Pillar II: Organizational Flexibility

The last few decades have seen a major shift in management structure, as America has moved from an economy dominated by big manufacturers to an economy dominated by the service sector and skilled knowledge workers. The old industrial and bureaucratic model was a pyramid, a many-layered hierarchy of managers with diminishing authority as the bottom was approached. Career paths were well defined: you started at the base of the pyramid and (hopefully) climbed up your appointed track toward the top. By contrast, the ideal organizational model for today's knowledge economy is flatter, with fewer layers of management and greater responsibility and authority for all workers. It is also more flexible; employees aren't confined to a specific career path but have much more control over their own professional development.

The willingness to experiment with flat and flexible organization structures is a common hallmark of Blue Sector firms. Blue companies are more likely to pare down layers of management, devolve responsibility to the lowest possible level, and break down the firewalls that separate top management from employees, fostering an egalitarian approach to day-to-day business. This encourages creativity in all employees, who know that their ideas can be more easily brought to the attention of the company's higher-ups. The business scholars Ori Brafman and Rod Beckstrom, in their recent book *The Starfish and the Spider,* emphasize the importance of decentralization in unleashing ingenuity.[11] It should be no surprise that progressive companies such as Apple and Google are among the best at figuring out how to harness the promise of decentralized organization. Brafman and Beckstrom's basic principle—"When you give people freedom, you get chaos, but you also get incredible creativity"[12]—is a tenet not only of flat organizations but also of the progressive movement as a whole, in society, politics, or business.

For example, although Google has become one of the fastest-growing, most influential companies in the world over the past few years, it retains much of the egalitarian ethos that guided it as a small start-up. *Forbes* described the company's open management style well: "this company loves to talk it out, jettisoning hierarchy, business silos and layers of management for a flatter, 'networked' structure where the guy with the best data wins."[13] Sergey Brin and Larry Page, the cofounders of Google, host a companywide Q&A session online on most Friday afternoons, where any employee can offer suggestions or ask questions.

The company does its work through small, focused, self-driving teams, using far fewer managers than the industry norm: "one for every 20 line employees, compared with one for as few as 7 industrywide."[14] This willingness to free employees from management control also plays a direct part in the company's outstanding record of innovation. Google employees are told to spend 20 percent of their time working freely on projects that interest them, "a practice that has already resulted in such Google innovations as Google News, Gmail, Google Talk, Orkut, and Froogle."[15] In its first year on the S&P 500, Google beat the index by 14.5 percent. Our research indicates that 100 percent of Google executives' political contributions over the last decade have gone to Democrats.

Whole Foods Market, another company whose top three executives have given 100 percent of their major-party contributions to Democrats, has an innovative management structure that devolves as much decision-making power as possible to the shop floor staff. The workforce at each Whole Foods grocery store is divided into teams that are responsible for a particular job and share in any extra profits generated by their team's productivity. The teams meet regularly to discuss and solve any problems in their unit. Any newly hired team member must be accepted by a two-thirds vote of the whole team; team members are better placed than managers to notice slackers who might bring down the team's performance (and profitability).[16]

This structure of self-motivating, largely self-managing teams allows Whole Foods to devolve authority to the level where people are most affected by the decision and best qualified to assess the issues at stake. In 2003, for example, the company held an all-employee vote on its benefits plan, on the principle that "Health insurance is the decision that frontline employees care most about, and whose elements they can most effectively judge." [17] Whole Foods put the entire benefits package (including medical plans and vacation time) up for vote by the company's 25,000 employees. In three rounds of voting with an 87 percent turnout rate, employees chose their favorite plan, which the company implemented. [18] Whole Foods, incidentally, is egalitarian not only in its decision making but also in its pay scale, where executives' salaries are limited to 14 times the pay of store workers. [19]

The nation's top organic grocer isn't the only big blue retailer that has managed to decentralize decision-making responsibilities to hundreds of nationwide branches. Bed Bath & Beyond (whose executives are 95 percent Democratic donors) has set itself apart from other "big-box" retailers by the power it delegates to its individual store managers, who are authorized to select 70 percent of the merchandise in their store and can thus adapt to distinctive local tastes and needs. [20] Thanks to this devolution of responsibility, Bed Bath & Beyond has strongly distinguished itself from other big-box stores while keeping up solid operating margins.

Blue companies tend to be flexible as well as flat; their employees enjoy not only upward but lateral mobility, finding a place in the company that fits their skills and lifestyles. Internal flexibility helps ensure that a corporation can capitalize on opportunities and avoid the pitfalls presented by a complex and rapidly shifting business landscape.

One quintessential example of such flexibility is Progressive's tradition of reorganizing regularly, formulated during former CEO Peter Lewis's tenure. Progressive employees change jobs and functions every two years according to their interests and strengths. This notion of perpetual change not only reflects the dynamics of the insurance market but also emphasizes the importance of bringing new people and perspectives to each segment of the company's business. As Lewis has noted, this kind of flexibility has been integral to the company's success: "You can't innovate if your culture won't let you take risks or do something different, or [doesn't] continuously demand from you new ideas and free thinking. I have a theory that if we don't reorganize internally annually, we'll probably be behind the curve."[21] Thanks in part to its flexible structure, Progressive has stayed ahead of the curve on everything from marketing to motorcycle insurance. Over the last ten years, it has outpaced the S&P 500 by a respectable 7.6 percent.

Pillar III: Ecoefficiency

Environmental impact is one of the classic areas where companies' economic interests are thought to clash with their social responsibility. Business and industry account for the lion's share of the world's pollution, greenhouse gas emissions, and consumption of natural resources (energy, water, air, fuel, and raw materials); plenty of ecologically damaging behavior is highly profitable. Perhaps surprisingly, however, environmental responsibility is also one of the few areas where business scholars have shown a clear connection between corporate virtue and financial success.

As mentioned in the last chapter, academics have argued back and forth for decades over whether corporate social responsibility is good for business or is a neutral factor. Today there's a growing consensus that at least one social responsibility factor is demonstrably connected to financial success: *ecoefficiency,* or "the economic value a company creates relative to the waste it generates."[22] Several recent stock market studies have concluded that ecoefficient companies tend to financially outperform their less responsible competitors.[23] Industry by industry, and in the U.S. economy as a whole, companies generally do better when they reduce their consumption of resources and their generation of waste. A recent Goldman Sachs analysis suggested that the "Eco-Efficiency Premium" in financial markets may in fact be increasing as environmental factors "are more appropriately priced," drawing investors' attention.[24]

The affinity between progressive values and environmental responsibility hardly needs to be spelled out, so it will come as no surprise that the Blue Sector includes many of America's most environmentally friendly companies. One blue pioneer in corporate ecoefficiency is the sports and fitness giant Nike, which has over the past decade sent 55 percent of its political spending to Democrats. In 1993, the company established a Nike Environmental Action Team (NEAT) whose mission was "to study Nike's operations through the emerging lens of sustainability, asking questions that would ultimately transform the company's understanding of itself and its mission."[25]

NEAT soon encountered the ideas of William McDonough, an architect and environmental consultant who advocates a "cradle-to-cradle" sustainability paradigm for product design. McDonough's proposals are extraordinarily daring—ultimately aiming at nothing less than the elimination of waste in industrial production—but are also solidly grounded in the realities of materials science. He begins at the product design stage (the first "cradle") and tries to ensure that every chemical and component that goes into a product either is biodegradable or can be perpetually recovered and used to make new products (the second "cradle"). As a *Forbes* profile put it, McDonough envisions "a world where everything industry churns out can either be composted, reused or recycled into something else."[26]

On the recommendation of NEAT, Nike formed a partnership with McDonough to assess the chemistry of all the materials used in its footwear and identify a "palette" of ingredients that fit the cradle-to-cradle paradigm. The company has committed to use only ingredients from that palette in its footwear production by the year 2020. Nike has been collecting and recycling used shoes since 1993—the shoe material generally goes into athletic surfaces and flooring—but in the future it intends to offer new shoes made from 100 percent recyclable or biodegradable materials, and to eliminate toxic chemicals from the production process. It's a scientifically demanding challenge, but Nike has prided itself on its inventiveness ever since cofounder Bill Bowerman came up with the superior "waffle sole" for Nike's original running shoe.[27]

In fact, Nike just overcame a similar environmental problem through technical ingenuity after more than a decade of research. Throughout the 1990s, its famous air-cushioned soles were partly filled with a buoyant, leak-resistant gas called sulfur hexafluoride, or SF6. Unfortunately, SF6 is a greenhouse gas far more potent than carbon dioxide, and in 1992 Nike became aware that its discarded shoes might have a startlingly significant effect on the climate. "At the peak of SF6 production in 1997, Nike Air footwear carried a greenhouse effect equivalent to an astonishing 7 million metric tons of carbon dioxide—about as much as the tailpipes of 1 million cars."[28]

Instead of denying or ignoring its contribution to climate change, Nike began hunting for a solution. Its researchers soon identified nitrogen gas as a possible substitute, but it would take almost fourteen years, millions of research dollars, and a total reengineering of the sole before the company found a way to make nitrogen cushion a runner's foot as effectively as SF6 did. The research had a major, unforeseen bonus, however: the shoe's new structure allowed Nike to fill the entire sole with air, not just the heel. The resulting Air Max shoe has been a huge commercial hit, richly rewarding Nike for phasing out SF6 in all its products. Sometimes it really does pay to do the right thing. Indeed, the success of the Blue Sector suggests that it pays more often than not.

Another blue company that has earned both praise and profits by its ecoefficiency is Johnson Controls, recently picked by *Forbes* as one of the 400 best big companies in America and by *Business Ethics* as one of the 100 best corporate citizens.[29] Though hardly a household name, Johnson Controls got its start in 1885 with what is today a common household product: the electric room thermostat, invented by its founder, Warren Johnson. Ever since, Johnson Controls has been a leading designer of climate control systems for buildings. In the late 1970s, it branched out into car batteries and interiors, which now provide more than half its revenue.

What unites these seemingly unrelated areas is the company's passion (and remarkable ingenuity) for energy efficiency. In both building and car design, Johnson Controls has pushed relentlessly for less waste, more use of recycled materials, and conservation of energy. Its automatic climate control systems are fine-tuned to heat and cool a building exactly where and when necessary, rather than wasting power by bringing an entire office to a uniform temperature. Johnson pioneered Personal Environment technology, which allows individuals to adjust the temperature, lighting, air flow, and acoustics of their own workspace.[30] Its building designs use natural light and water-conserving plumbing systems. In a new building, Johnson's control systems and other devices "can cut energy bills by 10% to 80%, depending on how many gadgets a client buys."[31] On the automotive side, despite being the largest producer of lead-acid car batteries in America, Johnson has managed to reduce its lead emissions by 59 percent since 1994 while increasing its battery production by 74 percent.[32] It uses recycled materials extensively in its car interior designs. Recently, it has become a major player in the market for hybrid car batteries, exploring innovative lithium-ion options.

Not surprisingly, Johnson Controls has stacked up an impressive array of environmental awards and recognitions. The EPA has honored Johnson for making cleaner car batteries, more fuel-efficient vehicle designs, and more energy-efficient buildings. The World Environment Center gave the company a gold medal for its emissions reductions, and energy-saving measures.[33] Johnson worked with the U.S. Green Building Council to develop the Leadership in Energy and Environmental Design (LEED) ratings system for efficient building design.[34] Two of Johnson's buildings in its Milwaukee headquarters have since earned LEED certification. Finally, the company has been rewarded with financial success. Not only has Johnson paid dividends every year since 1887, but its shareowners have enjoyed an unbroken string of annual dividend increases since 1975, and its stock has done 13.8 percent better than the S&P 500 over the last ten years.[35] Despite the need for government access, Johnson has sent 51 percent of its political spending to Democrats in the past decade.

Ecoefficiency doesn't often make headlines because even its milestones tend to be incremental changes that impress only when the total impact is added up. For example, blue company

Starbucks worked for a decade with its suppliers and the advocacy group Environmental Defense to develop a coffee cup from recycled paper.[36] Its research paid off in 2004 with the first ever FDA approval for recycled material in food packaging. This may seem like a small thing, but it is expected to reduce the Seattle-based coffee company's environmental footprint by 5 million pounds of tree fiber a year.[37] Starbucks has also been a leader in pushing its franchisees to use water and energy efficiently in their retail stores. Like Starbucks' famously generous employee benefits policy, these measures were derided as unprofitable by conservative critics, yet the company continues to thrive. In the last five election cycles, Starbucks' top three executives have given more than 95 percent of their political contributions to Democrats.

Though no oil company passes the bar to get into the Blue Sector, there are several blue utilities with positive environmental records. Consider FPL Energy, an electric utility firm that operates the world's largest solar fields and is the United States' leading wind energy developer. According to Innovest Strategic Value Advisors, a socially responsible investment analysis firm, FPL is the best environmental performer in the utility sector (out of 28 power companies rated).[38] It was one of the first American utilities to commit to 100 percent clean energy production by 2050 and to support a regulatory cap on carbon dioxide emissions. FPL has also been widely praised for its innovative programs to reuse industrial wastewater and protect wetland, river, and ocean ecosystems. Unlike most utilities, FPL has no PAC; its executives have contributed 100 percent to Democrats, and its stock price has outpaced the S&P 500 by 8.7 percent over the past ten years.

A large share of blue companies have received EPA recognition for their positive environmental impact. Whole Foods has received the Green Power Leadership Award for meeting 100 percent of its energy needs from clean and renewable sources (biomass, geothermal, small hydroelectric plants, solar power, and wind).[39] Cell phone chip maker Qualcomm, which leads its industry in America, was recently praised by the EPA for its commuter policies. The company provides public transportation subsidies, hybrid shuttle buses, and bike lockers to encourage workers to choose an environmentally friendly method of commuting.[40] Qualcomm sends 66 percent of its political contributions to Democrats, and its stock has beaten the market by 25.1 percent over the last ten years.

Overall, it's no surprise that environmentally responsible companies are more likely to contribute to ecofriendly politicians. Unlike some large corporations (say, Exxon Mobil, Dow Chemical, and Ford), their executives haven't embraced a business strategy that depends on lax government regulation. Instead, blue companies are more likely to deal with environmental challenges through relentless innovation and waste reduction. The data clearly link these sorts of forward-thinking environmental policies with business success. In an era of expensive oil and gas, we can expect ecoefficient companies to have an ever-growing advantage.

CHAPTER 5

The Principles of Progressive Leadership II

Dealing with Employees, Critics, and the Long Haul

ONE OF THE GREAT LIMITATIONS OF THE CONSER-
vative notion of business is a fearful, adversarial view of everything that isn't a corporation. From a right-wing ideological
perspective, employees constantly threaten company profits
with their demands for better pay, benefits, pensions, and job
security (even when they don't manage to form a union). Public
interest groups are insatiable critics that will only escalate their
costly demands on a company that responds to their complaints.
The government is an authoritarian monster, strangling business with red tape, regulation, and taxes. (At least according to
the ideology. In reality, plenty of conservative companies look to
the government as a source of fat, easy profits and get away with
paying very little in taxes.)

Fear and aggression were the explicit bases for the Powell
Memorandum. Lewis Powell believed that organized labor and

Ralph Nader's public interest groups were making war on the American way of life, and in Powell's 1971 manifesto we can see the model for the typical red company response to such critics. Business should not shrink from "guerrilla warfare with those who propagandize against the system." "There should not be the slightest hesitation to press vigorously in all political arenas for support of the enterprise system. Nor should there be reluctance to penalize politically those who oppose it."[1]

More than three decades later, the conservative machine has built up a powerful defensive front to resist demands from employees and advocacy groups. Red companies are well versed in union bashing and cutting back on worker-related costs. Right-wing think tanks, media outlets, and paid experts are prepared to drown out any environmental or human rights group that might challenge Republican policy. The Bush White House and the GOP Congress have done their best to gut the institutions that are meant to keep a critical eye on corporate behavior, from the EPA to the National Labor Relations Board. Like Lewis Powell, much of the Right has mistaken criticism for socialism. They see American business as fragile and under threat—and they are convinced that the solution is to take a strong stand against all enemies, including, in some cases, labor unions and employees.

> **Myth: To stay profitable, corporations must maintain an adversarial relationship with their workers—and certainly with progressive advocacy groups.**

Progressive CEOs don't buy into this myth. They are confident instead of defensive, collaborative instead of antagonistic.

Instead of treating employees and advocacy groups as enemies, Blue Sector business leaders tend to treat them as partners in the essential process of developing fair and sustainable business practices.

Last chapter, we discussed how innovation flows from a particular, progressive type of corporate culture. Business leaders who want to innovate in the field of socially responsible business need to foster a culture of collaboration with workers and with progressive issue groups. Want to make it onto *Fortune*'s list of the 100 Best Companies to Work For? Listen to what your workers need, and look at the blue companies that have successfully built an employee-centric corporate culture. Want to distinguish yourself as an ethical alternative in a crowded market or simply save money by being more ecoefficient? Partner with a labor rights or environmental group that can show you how to do it right.

The conservatives' defensiveness is tied to their destructive short-term focus. In the short run, companies that treat their workers badly and shut out criticism can make a profit, but over the long haul, companies that invest in their workforce and turn critics into partners are more likely to thrive. All the other pillars are summed up in the final pillar of progressive leadership: a long-term vision.

Reality: Blue companies thrive by investing in their employees and working constructively with critics, all as part of a long-term perspective on business success.

Pillar IV: Investment in Employees' Well-being

Companies that "act blue" are, by definition, more likely to adhere to fair labor standards, offer expansive benefit packages, and believe in the strength of diversity. Many Blue Sector companies don't just get a passing grade on this test; they truly distinguish themselves by their creative commitment to employee welfare. Unlike many of their red counterparts, they don't see proper treatment of workers solely as a drain on profits. Rather, they recognize that investing in all of their employees builds a strong long-term foundation for their businesses.

Plenty of red company CEOs are happy to invest in the white-collar professional staff at headquarters but treat their low-wage shop or factory floor workforce as a commodity where cutting costs is the overriding goal. These companies pay low wages, provide the minimum possible benefit levels, and don't encourage their workers to stick around for too long. Many of the biggest Blue Sector companies, by contrast, have put tremendous energy and imagination into investing in their blue-collar and low-skilled workers. They are more likely to refer to all their employees as "partners" or "team members" and to back up that inclusive language with a genuine team mentality, as evidenced by policies that benefit and empower their workers at every level.

Take Starbucks, which is well known for defying the low-benefits trend in the service sector. The multinational coffee franchise not only pays higher wages than its industry rivals but also grants health insurance and stock options to every Starbucks employee ("partner") who works more than twenty hours per week. Providing health coverage to part-time employees is virtually unheard of in the food service industry. Fast-food restaurants, their lobbyists, and their front groups, such as the Employment Policies Institute,[2] have poured tremendous energy into fighting increases in mandatory wage or benefit levels for low-wage workers. Their efforts helped keep the federal minimum wage stuck at $5.15 for nearly a decade and in 1998 got "McJob" into the *Oxford English Dictionary*: "An unstimulating, low-paid job with few prospects, esp. one created by the expansion of the service sector."[3]

If you look only at the immediate cost consequences, the McJobs bare-minimum model seems to make sense. A whopping 65 percent of Starbucks' 100,000-plus American employees are eligible for insurance under the company's current, generous policy. Starbucks spends more on health care than it does on coffee.[4] Yet the company has benefited tremendously from higher employee morale and retention rates. In a *BusinessWeek* interview, Starbucks Chairman Howard Schultz noted that his company has "probably the lowest rate of attrition of any retailer in America." Other food service companies have, in Schultz's words, "used employee churn as a mechanism to keep wages low and health insurance out of the labor picture."[5] Starbucks, by contrast, was willing to bet that the hidden costs of employee churn were greater than the costs of investing in a dedicated, loyal workforce.

The company's bet has paid off. According to a study by the Tuck School of Business at Dartmouth College, Starbucks has an annual turnover rate of 60 percent—significantly lower than the food service industry average of 200 percent—which reduces the cost and inefficiency of having to hire and train new workers every few months. In addition, when asked by external surveyors, 82 percent of Starbucks employees claim to be "very satisfied" with their jobs, an astonishingly high rate not only for the fast food sector but for any large company.[6] In a business where customer service is all-important, that kind of high morale on the front lines is an intangible but vital asset. By refusing to compromise on its progressive culture, Starbucks has gone from strength to strength, outperforming the S&P 500 by 15.9 percent over the past ten years.

For a similar example, look at America's number one warehouse retailer, Costco Wholesale Corporation. Jim Sinegal, the CEO and cofounder of Costco, is a low-cost crusader. His warehouse stores are pared down to the minimum: concrete floors, simple wooden shelving, skylights instead of electric lighting. Sinegal relentlessly wrangles the lowest bulk rates from his suppliers on everything from Starbucks coffee to pricey Coach handbags and passes most of those cost savings on to consumers. Despite pressure from Wall Street analysts, Sinegal refuses to nickel-and-dime away the wide margin between Costco's markups on goods (14 to 15 percent) and the retail industry norm (25 to 50 percent). "When I started, Sears, Roebuck was the Costco of the country, but they allowed someone else to come in under them," Sinegal explained in a *New York Times* interview.[7] Instead of asking what price increases Costco can charge, he maintains an unyielding focus on pushing prices lower.

When it comes to his company's more than 113,000 employees, however, Sinegal applies the same stubbornness to the opposite principle. Hourly wages at Costco are on average 42 percent higher than those paid by Sam's Club, its closest competitor in the warehouse retail business. Costco is also far more generous than the retail industry average in its benefit package and in the amount it pays toward its employees' health care costs and 401(k) plans.[8] Sinegal has resisted pressure to whittle away at those generous margins, too, sticking to his mantra that good wages lead to "good people and good productivity."[9] He doesn't want to experiment with seeing what wage and benefit cuts Costco can get away with before morale and productivity begin to suffer.

Sinegal's main concession to keeping wage costs low is capping his own salary at twelve times that of the lowest-paid Costco employee. In sharp contrast to the ego-driven CEOs of many comparable large firms, his no-frills employment contract is devoid of corporate perks. To Sinegal, anything else would be hypocrisy: "I just think that if you're going to try to run an organization that's very cost-conscious, then you can't have those disparities. Having an individual who is making 100 or 200 or 300 times more than the average person working on the floor is wrong."[10]

Costco is often compared with the red giant Wal-Mart, which owns Sam's Club and is likewise famous for its low-cost retail paradigm. A key ingredient of Wal-Mart's business model, however, is keeping employees' wages and benefits as low as possible—at least for the ground troops. Wal-Mart executives take home a dramatically higher salary than Sinegal, while many of its shop floor employees fall below the poverty line and have to rely on food stamps and other government aid to survive.[11] Not surprisingly, Wal-Mart is one of America's strongest antiunion forces, preferring to close a store rather than see its workers organize. Costco, by contrast, has a warmly constructive relationship with its unions. Rome Aloise, head of the Teamsters local that represents Costco workers, told *USA Today* that the company was so generous that "it almost scares me."[12]

We've heard similar sentiments from other union heads when we tell them about the Blue Sector; even labor leaders have absorbed the conservative dogma that union-friendly companies will suffer for their generosity to workers. Aloise didn't need to worry. A 2004 *BusinessWeek* survey found that "Costco's high-wage approach" outperformed the rival model of Sam's Club. Thanks to "lower turnover and higher productivity," the survey found, "the 102,000 Sam's employees in the U.S. generated some $35 billion in sales last year, while Costco did $34 billion with one-third fewer employees."[13] Over the last decade, Costco's shares have outpaced the S&P 500 by 7.1 percent. Costco is also thoroughly blue, with 98 percent of its executives' political contributions going to Democrats over the past five election cycles. In a recent *BusinessWeek* article, Sinegal welcomed Costco's inclusion on the Blue Index.[14]

In highly cost-competitive industries, Blue Sector CEOs look for ways to boost worker productivity other than slashing wages and benefits. Take Sidney Harman, an exemplary progressive leader in society and politics as well as in business: he was active in the 1960s civil rights movement, served as an undersecretary of commerce in the Carter administration, and is married to a Democratic member of Congress. Throughout his five-decade business career in the audio industry, Harman has been driving innovation on multiple fronts. Technologically, as a founder of Harman Kardon in the 1950s, he was a pioneer in designing the first high-performance home audio equipment that actually looked like furniture, not machinery. He's also been responsible for several successful experiments in participatory management, putting his Ph.D. in social psychology to use in building employee-centric factories and workplaces.[15]

His current company, Harman International Industries, has for twenty-seven years been a thriving manufacturer of high-end audio equipment. In a fiercely competitive industry, Harman has kept an edge thanks to its employee-centric culture, which fully integrates workers into the all-important project of building their own productivity. Any Harman employee who suggests a productivity-increasing measure gets to share in the profits generated by that measure. Workers don't need to worry that heightened productivity will cost them their jobs, because the company puts effort into identifying "off-line enterprises"—useful employment for workers who become redundant in a temporary slump or because of increased productivity. Harman also takes a hands-on approach to building up its low-skilled workforce by providing in-house English and mathematics courses to all of its factory workers. The result, over the last ten years, has been Harman's stock outrunning the S&P 500 by a whopping 21.7 percent; the company's performance earned it a place among the "Best Stocks of the Millennium" in 2006.[16] Over the last decade, Harman International's executives have given 99 percent of their political donations to Democrats.

Harman shows how the whole-company "team" or "partner" mentality goes beyond higher wages and more generous benefits. Blue Sector firms are better at getting every employee to engage with the mission of the company through profit-sharing measures and institutionalized incentives for innovation. At Google, for example, a twenty-seven-year-old engineer, Niniane Wang, received a million-dollar "founders' award" in 2004 for her work in developing Google Desktop. These generous innovation incentives aren't limited to the software development side of the company. As Google cofounder Sergey Brin has said, "The fact that we are fairly engineering-centric has been misinterpreted to mean that somehow the other functions are less important. The fact is that we want everybody in the company to be innovative. You can see that in our legal or financial work—with the IPO, for example—and with our compensation systems."[17]

In general, Google has made a name for itself by treating its workforce exceptionally well. It took the top slot on *Fortune*'s 2007 list of the 100 Best Companies to Work For.[18] The company offers an enviable slew of perquisites geared toward making its employees' lives more pleasant and balanced: free on-site gyms, laundry, and doctor's visits; a Wi-Fi–enabled shuttle bus; gourmet cafeterias serving healthy, free, and exceptionally tasty meals all day. Google employees can bring their pets to work and take care of errands while at work instead of leaving the Google campus to do them. The company even offers each employee $5,000 toward buying a hybrid car.

Not all of the Blue Sector companies on the *Fortune* list (which in 2007 also included Whole Foods, Qualcomm, Starbucks, Adobe Systems, Nike, Paychex, and Bright Horizons) offer their workers quite such an idyllic "university-style" habitat, but their benefits packages still tend to be both creative and generous. The software company Adobe Systems, for example, offers stock options to all employees, generous tuition reimbursement, employee counseling, and three weeks' paid sabbatical for every five years of work. Gay and lesbian Adobe employees are entitled to health and dental coverage for their domestic partners. The company's headquarters includes not only a fitness center but also a farmer's market. Adobe's executives have given 100 percent of their contributions to Democrats in the last ten years, and over the same period the company's stock has performed 17.6 percent better than the S&P 500.

Small or midsized technology companies can generally afford to treat their staff well, but despite the challenges of a huge and growing workforce with a great number of low-skilled jobs, Whole Foods has also been on *Fortune*'s list of Best Companies to Work For ever since the magazine started publishing it (up at number 5 in 2007).[19] Like Starbucks, Whole Foods has extraordinary levels of employee satisfaction and productivity. It offers generous health benefits, as you'd expect from a benefits package that was chosen in a companywide vote. In addition to generous wage levels, the worker teams in each store share in the profits from their increased productivity, giving every employee a real stake in the company's success. As a result of its committed workforce, Whole Foods' stock value has increased sixfold since 2000—which is even sweeter for its employees, because 93 percent of the company's stock options have gone to ordinary Whole Foods workers, including part-timers.[20]

Pillar V: Constructive Relationships with Critics

Another crucial area of blue company strength is forming cooperative, mutually beneficial relationships with progressive critics. This cuts against the grain not only of big business but also of human nature. Defensiveness and hostility are the natural human responses to criticism, so it's no surprise that relationships between major multinational companies and progressive advocacy groups are usually adversarial. No CEO likes to be told that his or her behavior is wrecking the environment, hollowing out local communities, or hurting impoverished farmers and workers abroad—especially when significant profits are at stake.

Most business leaders see activists as an encumbrance to be handled by PR spin, rather than interested parties whose ideas deserve a fair hearing. This trend is exacerbated by conservative think tanks like the American Enterprise Institute and the Federalist Society, which constantly pump out hostile propaganda about the excessive political influence of "unaccountable," "unelected" nongovernmental organizations (NGOs). Of course,

AEI and the Federalist Society are themselves NGOs, accountable only to their largely corporate funders, and both enjoy tremendous political clout.[21] But their anti-NGO messages have contributed to an atmosphere where companies see criticism from progressive groups as a threat, not an opportunity.

In fact, cooperative relationships with advocacy groups offer a huge benefit. In a global market where the health of a company's brand is all-important, there are great advantages to building a corporate reputation for active social responsibility. Blue company CEOs are more likely to seize these advantages, overcoming their defensiveness and recognizing advocacy groups as partners in developing a progressive business model. Any survey of the Blue Sector will turn up plenty of cases where blue companies openly acknowledged criticism from progressive groups and collaborated with those groups to find mutually acceptable solutions to seemingly intractable problems.

For example, along with the acceleration of globalization since the early 1990s, we have seen the growth of a powerful antisweatshop movement. Labor rights advocates in America and Europe have protested the terrible working conditions in many poor-country factories: sixteen-hour work days in filthy, overheated spaces; exposure to hazardous chemicals; sick or pregnant workers fired for leaving the work site; starvation wages; violent repression of union activity. Many of the offending factories are contractors for Western companies, which tend to select foreign suppliers based on price, not labor practices. The antisweatshop activist groups have challenged Western manufacturers and retailers to demand better behavior all the way up their supply chains.

The sweatshop issue has never been simple, of course. Western corporations can do only so much to uphold labor standards

in places like Indonesia or El Salvador, where the local government doesn't enforce those standards (or, as in the case of China
and Vietnam, forbids workers from forming independent unions
by law). If Western manufacturers pull their factories back to
developed countries with better labor protection, they will hurt
precisely the impoverished workers the antisweatshop campaigners are trying to protect. Some major multinational companies use these complexities as an excuse to stonewall and do
nothing. A number of blue companies, by contrast, have been
pioneers in the messy process of auditing their suppliers and
trying to ensure fair and healthy working conditions in overseas
factories.

Throughout the early 1990s, even fairly conscientious corporations responded to antisweatshop protests with defensive tactics.[22] Companies such as Nike and Gap Inc. (an 80 percent
Democratic company that owns Gap, Old Navy, and other
apparel retail brands), promised to strengthen their labor standards and carry out more frequent factory inspections, but they
held back from the two measures that would give their codes of
conduct genuine credibility: an independent auditing process
and transparent reporting of the results. Such measures would
have required real trust and willingness to cooperate with "the
enemy"—the advocacy groups calling for a boycott of Gap
clothes and Nike shoes. Who knew what the activists would do
with a full directory of supplier factories?

Eventually, however, the companies realized that no damage
control strategy could remove the "sweatshop" tarnish from
their brands. A handful of major blue companies went on to lead
a transparency revolution in the apparel industry. An early
groundbreaker was Liz Claiborne, another 80 percent Democratic donor, which in 1998 opened one of its major Guatemalan fac-

tories to the local activist group Coverco. The company widely publicized Coverco's resulting report, including the many embarrassing ways in which the factory failed to meet the company's code of conduct.[23] Liz Claiborne later worked closely with antisweatshop groups and other companies (including Nike) to create the Fair Labor Association, an independent monitoring organization that carries out random, unannounced audits of working conditions in the factories of its corporate members. For its part, Gap Inc. worked with the sweatshop monitoring group Verité and the Business Leaders Initiative on Human Rights (BLIHR), a consortium of businesses dedicated to finding solutions to difficult global labor issues.

In 2005, Nike and Gap both issued landmark corporate responsibility reports for the previous year, admitting the labor problems they had found in their overseas suppliers.[24] Both companies had worked with progressive advocacy groups acting as independent monitors; both had also set up their own internal labor-standard compliance departments with more than 90 employees. Gap had inspected 90.4 percent of its more than 2,600 suppliers and described with detail and candor the many code violations it discovered. In a pilot factory-rating project, the company gave individual ratings to its suppliers in six countries and reported that 38 percent of the sample factories needed remediation (18 percent urgently). Similarly, Nike found that 25 percent of its supplier factories got a "C" or "D" grade; the company lacked information to grade another 16 percent satisfactorily. In a final gesture that astonished its previous critics, Nike made public the names and addresses of its 700-plus supplier factories, allowing any activist or journalist to visit and check up on the working conditions.

Transparent monitoring is only a start, of course; it helps

everyone concerned understand the real scale of the problem and makes remediation possible. Nike and Gap work closely with suppliers that fail the test but are willing to change their ways, training their managers to increase productivity without abusing workers. In 2004, Gap revoked the contracts of seventy suppliers for major violations such as child labor or falsified records; for the most part, though, both companies do their best to fix factories rather than close them.

Thanks to their honesty and their ongoing efforts to improve their suppliers' practices, both Gap and Nike won recognition in 2006 from a wide range of progressive groups. Both companies made it onto *Business Ethics* magazine's annual list of 100 Best Corporate Citizens.[25] Gap won a Sustainability Reporting Award from Ceres, a leading organization in corporate social responsibility evaluation, which has praised Gap Inc.'s exceptional social reporting for the past several years.[26] In November 2006, Nike was rated the top U.S. company (and was in the top ten of world companies) for social responsibility reporting by the independent consultancy SustainAbility.[27]

The companies have benefited from more than just a burnished brand, however. Gap Vice President for Social Responsibility Dan Henkle is convinced that his company's conscientious policies have strengthened its supply chain. In his experience, socially responsible factories are not only morally preferable to sweatshops; they also tend to be more reliable in the quality of their goods, their delivery times, and their general business practices. "If you're running a good factory from a social responsibility standpoint, typically you're running a good factory on all other elements that are important to us as well," Henkle says. "And that makes sense to me. If you're a good manager and you're running a good operation, you're probably running a good operation on all fronts."[28] Over the last ten years, the stocks of Nike, Gap, and Liz Claiborne have outperformed the S&P 500 by modest margins.

Companies that aren't willing to open their supply chain to independent monitoring are less likely to know which of their suppliers are covering up flaws. Consider the big red company retailers Target Corporation and Wal-Mart, which have so far resisted any labor standards that might threaten their ability to get the cheapest goods possible. These retail giants insist that their in-house monitoring efforts are sufficient and refuse to collaborate with antisweatshop groups. Yet a *Business Week* exposé in November 2006 showed that Chinese factories were deceiving Wal-Mart and Target, using false records to conceal labor code violations.[29] Their inability to work with independent monitors leaves Wal-Mart and Target vulnerable to disasters that might damage their brand and weaken their supply chain.

Sweatshops aren't the only inconvenient truth that red companies would rather overlook. Nearly all American oil companies spent the last decade fervently denying the reality of climate change and maintained an antagonistic relationship with environmental groups. Blue company utilities like FPL Energy and PG&E have taken a more constructive tack, investing in alternative energy sources and working with major progressive groups like Environmental Defense and the Natural Resources Defense Council. These utilities were among the first major corporations to publicly call for a cap-and-trade system on carbon dioxide.[30] PG&E, the largest gas and electricity provider in California, has recently gone further by introducing a pioneering "carbon offset" program for its customers. Since early 2007, PG&E customers have been able to balance out their power consumption by sending money to restore or conserve California forests, which absorb and retain carbon dioxide. The voluntary program is estimated to cost the average power user a mere $4 per month.[31] PG&E, a 51 percent Democratic donor over the past decade, has figured out how to expand its business by working with advocacy groups. Meanwhile, red company skeptics about climate change such as Exxon Mobil, sensing that not only science but also public opinion and politics are against them, are belatedly and begrudgingly opening a dialogue with environmentalist groups.[32]

A constructive relationship with progressive critics is not the same thing as caving in. Since the late 1990s, Starbucks has attracted plenty of criticism and pressure from groups like Global Exchange that wanted it to market "fair-trade" coffees—beans from farmer cooperatives whose members receive a guaranteed price despite the fluctuations of the international coffee market. From its earliest days, Starbucks has helped coffee farmers by paying premium prices and funding development projects, and the company was open to the idea of fair trade. Starbucks was concerned, however, that fair-trade cooperatives would not be able to consistently produce enough of the high-quality coffee beans associated with its brand. It accordingly resisted activists' demands to start buying 5 percent of Starbucks coffee from fair-trade producers. Instead, in 2000 the company worked with the advocacy group TransFair USA to begin buying high-quality fair-trade beans in moderate quantities to test customer demand. Starbucks steadily increased its fair-trade purchases over the following years until, by 2005, the company was the single largest American importer of fair-trade beans, buying 11.5 million pounds of them (or 3.7 percent of the company's total coffee).[33]

At the same time, Starbucks has pushed to make the coffee industry as a whole more transparent. Critics of fair-trade groups have pointed out that groups such as TransFair USA approve only small democratic cooperatives, which represent a minute share of the overall coffee production market.[34] Starbucks pushes for transparency clauses in all its contracts, requiring its suppliers to show how much money actually goes to the farmers. In 2004, Starbucks introduced its Coffee and Farmer Equity (CAFE) standard, which, unlike fair-trade certification, applies to all coffee suppliers, however they are organized. Under CAFE, Starbucks gives preferential status to suppliers that receive a high score for their social and environmental practices, including fair compensation to farmworkers.[35] Starbucks also provides training and assistance for suppliers who want to comply with CAFE. It's an open question whether the fair trade movement or Starbucks' measures will have a positive impact on more coffee farmers, given that CAFE applies to a much broader swath of the coffee industry.

None of Starbucks' actions has entirely ended criticism of the company. Some of the shriller critics are hostile to Starbucks simply for being an omnipresent coffee corporation. Others wanted the company to market fair-trade beans even more aggressively. Consistent with its progressive corporate culture, Starbucks has responded constructively to critics who were willing to work with it. The company has been careful, however, to act in ways that protect its reputation for quality. It remains widely recognized as both a good corporation and a good place to buy coffee.

Pillar VI: Long-Term Perspective

One final hallmark of progressive companies—and progressive CEOs—is their intense interest in building the long-term fundamentals of a successful business. Rather than focusing exclusively on the short-term demands of Wall Street, blue companies' leaders tend to focus on building customer loyalty, growing their businesses at a sustainable, healthy pace, and ensuring that good corporate governance standards (and not cronyism) define their businesses' day-to-day operations.

This insistence on taking the long view is really an ethos infusing all the other pillars. Companies that plan to be around for the long haul prioritize things like ecoefficiency and investing in their workforce, even if they seem to increase their costs in the short term. Many Blue Sector CEOs are company founders and think of their position as a lifetime vocation, not just as a bunch of stock options and a golden parachute. Blue company leaders are more likely to set goals and incentives over a five-, ten-, or twenty-year time frame.

Of course, every corporate executive claims to be thinking of the long term, but most are soon dragged into chasing quarterly targets. After taking his company public in 1992, Bed Bath & Beyond's cofounder Warren Eisenberg found himself under constant pressure from Wall Street to boost short-term profits. He kept his company strong by ignoring those calls. "When we were private we didn't plan the profits. We just did everything we thought was right, and the profits were always there. We still do everything that we think is right, long term and short term, and it comes out right."[36]

Costco founder and CEO Jim Sinegal sees things the same way. Though many analysts have insisted that Costco could increase its profitability by driving down wages, Sinegal sees this as a short-term, self-defeating approach to business. "Wall Street is in the business of making money between now and next Tuesday. We're in the business of building an organization, an institution that we hope will be here 50 years from now. And paying good wages and keeping your people working with you is very good business."[37]

Profit is at the heart of corporate success, of course, but executives who make the financial bottom line their top priority tend to get sidetracked into short-term thinking. Many of the most successful blue companies have thrived by focusing first on their long-term identity as a company—their core concept, the one thing they do best—with profit as an important but secondary consideration. Apple is one of the strongest examples. Under the direction of founder and CEO Steve Jobs, it has continually gone in new directions; back in 1984, when Apple released its Super Bowl ad for the new Macintosh, who would have imagined that the company would one day revolutionize the music industry? At the same time, Apple has kept a consistent corporate identity: innovative, consumer-focused, with a high priority on user-friendliness and cutting-edge design. Its impressive profits have flowed consistently from focus on its core identity.

Whole Foods cofounder and CEO John Mackey uses happiness as an analogy for the relationship between a long-term vision and long-term profits:

> In my life experience happiness is best experienced by not aiming for it directly. A person who focuses their life energies strictly on striving for their own self-interest and personal happiness is often someone who is also a narcissist, someone who is self-involved and obsessed with their own ego gratification. . . .
>
> [Similarly, in] my business experience, profits are best achieved by not making them the primary goal of

the business. Rather, long-term profits are the result of having a deeper business purpose, great products, customer satisfaction, employee happiness, excellent suppliers, community and environmental responsibility—these are the keys to maximizing long-term profits. The paradox of profits is that, like happiness, they are best achieved by not aiming directly for them.[38]

It's no surprise that the Blue Sector has a high share of business leaders who understand the power of a long-term vision. Over the last decade, the executives of blue companies have given the majority of their political contributions to a party that has been largely shut out of power. These are precisely the kind of managers who are likely to lead based on a vision, not on the chance for short-term profit. These progressive leaders take pride in what their company stands for, not just in the size of their compensation packages.

This kind of farsighted approach distinguishes not only progressive companies but also progressive government from the competition. We've said it a few times already, but it bears saying again: the Republican Party has turned itself into the party of short-term gratification and long-term disaster. The current government has touted tax cuts without concern for deficits, pushed wasteful and destructive environmental policies, ignored the consequences of oil dependency, and done its best to shortchange American workers and the middle class by dismantling their safety net. By contrast, great political leaders and great CEOs alike succeed by planning for the long term. They strive for sustainability, foster innovation, and invest in their people and their reputation.

In a market where roughly 80 percent of the largest companies support the Republican Party and its candidates, the 76 constituents of the Blue Index show us that companies with progressive values can not only match but also exceed their more conservative counterparts. By creating strong, loyal, and effective workforces, encouraging progressive thinking, and embracing progressive leadership, these companies have been able to achieve strong financial and social returns—and have done so while maintaining their position among the world's biggest companies.

PART II

The Blue Manifesto

CHAPTER 6

Buying Blue

A Guide for the Awakened Consumer

UP TO THIS POINT, WE'VE DONE OUR BEST TO PRES-
ent the evidence for a distinctively progressive way of doing
business—a way that's good for the economy, good for the environment, good for workers, and good for America. We've high-
lighted the companies that have thrived by internalizing
progressive values. The Blue Sector is real. Unfortunately, the
Blue Sector is also small.

We'd be overjoyed if our analysis alone had an impact on red
company CEOs—if the figures and stories we've collected
would awaken them to the power of progressive leadership,
helping to correct the partisan bias of corporate America. We
certainly hope this book changes a few minds on Wall Street.
But we know that old prejudices die hard, especially when
they're reinforced by the majority of other American corporate
leaders and an entrenched Republican propaganda machine. A
lot of very powerful people with an interest in defending the status quo have passed through the revolving doors between corpo-

rate boardrooms, right-wing think tanks, lobbying organizations, and Republican cabinet positions.

As we said back in Chapter 1, business leaders aren't going to pay too much attention to a couple of Democrats writing a book, but they will pay attention to their consumers and shareholders. Back in 1971, Lewis Powell made a big splash with his manifesto addressed to "top management" and the U.S. Chamber of Commerce. With our Blue Manifesto, we are aiming a little lower. Shareholders are the real owners of American business; consumers have unmatched power to sway corporate decisions. Powell wanted to awaken corporate America to its political power. We want to awaken progressives to their power over corporate America.

The Network Versus the Machine

Powell's key insight was correct: to succeed in politics, you need to create an infrastructure that mobilizes money behind your values. The conservative side took to this lesson enthusiastically. They won over enough billionaires and CEOs to create a deep, liquid political capital market and leveraged their existing money to bring in ever more corporate cash. The money shored up their political infrastructure—the media outlets, policy think tanks, legal institutes, grassroots mobilization campaigns, and so on. Through a combination of relentless propaganda and political hardball, they did their best to turn both Wall Street and K Street into fully owned subsidiaries of the Republican Party.

Because the Republican machine was based on a flawed ideology, it inevitably culminated in corruption. Money and power are corrupting forces on either side of the political spectrum, but the Republicans took the fast lane to sleaze by embracing the dogma that oversight and regulation were inherently bad. It didn't help that they built their infrastructure around loyal lobbyists who doubled as partisan fund-raisers, or that they fostered a culture of secrecy in Congress and the White House. The challenge for progressives is to muster money behind their values and build a competitive, twenty-first-century political infrastructure without falling into similar corrupt practices.

Some progressive Americans have grown so disillusioned with big business that they question whether it's even possible to separate corporate money from sleaze. We need to be careful not to end up in a mental trap like the Republicans, who ever since Barry Goldwater have been quick to trot out a litany of all the ways that "government" screws things up in America. Plenty of right-wing anecdotes about government blunders and abuses are totally fabricated, but some are true. Wherever power is concentrated, some people will use it clumsily or unethically.

By focusing on the abuses and blowing them out of honest proportion, however, Republicans have blinded themselves to the tremendous benefits of democratic government. No other institution can be relied on to correct market failures or provide essential services to the whole population. The American government is ultimately accountable to the people. When it goes wrong, the answer isn't to shrink it "to the size where it can be drowned in the bathtub," in the memorable phrase of the right-wing strategist Grover Norquist. The democratic (and Democratic) answer is for American citizens to wake up, come together, and reclaim their government from incompetent or corrupt politicians. The U.S. government belongs to us, and we're responsible for keeping it honest.

In the same way, we progressive Americans must not let corporate abuses blind us to the goodness of the private sector. We know from the success of the Blue Sector that progressive values are compatible with a thriving market economy that produces plenty of jobs, wealth, and rising living standards. When a corporation makes a profit while compensating its employees fairly, protecting the environment, and respecting human rights, we should all cheer. When companies behave unethically, we shouldn't write off all of corporate America as irredeemably corrupt. Instead, we need to hold unscrupulous executives accountable, reward socially responsible businesses, and (in cases where the problem is systemic) press for appropriate government regulations. Ultimately, the U.S. economy belongs to us as well, and we have the power to change it.

What does that power look like? We believe it stems from informed, awakened citizens and a diverse ecosystem of progressive organizations, organized in an emerging political network. Because this network is based on the principles of progressive leadership, it will resist corruption better than the centralized conservative political machine. When the Republican leadership in Congress and the White House institutionalized corporate bribery as the basis for lawmaking, the rot spread quickly with only scattered murmurs of dissent from within the conservative ranks. By contrast, the new progressive network benefits from a nonhierarchical organizational structure, openness to criticism, and a set of values that prioritize long-term sustainability over short-term profit. Millions of progressive individuals and thousands of progressive organizations are its watchdogs. Even if one part should fall victim to corruption, other groups will be on hand to analyze, criticize, and keep the movement headed in the right direction.

Every individual progressive can contribute to this movement. After all, we are all consumers. At some point in the past year, most of us have bought goods or services from one of the companies mentioned in this book. Corporate America depends on us for its livelihood. That provides a key opportunity for us to challenge its political bias.

It's time for progressives to fully incorporate our political values into our daily lives. We have always believed that personal decisions matter on the national stage—at least if you listen to the long history of progressive slogans: "Think globally, act locally." "The personal is political." "Be the change you want to see in the world." But just like socially responsible investors, conscientious consumers have focused on companies' obvious environmental and social behavior while averting their eyes from their political behavior. If we're going to apply consumer pressure to reverse the political bias of American business, serious progressives need to start "buying blue."

The good news is, it's easy to shift your consumer spending in a blue direction. Despite great efforts by companies to disguise their political spending, we have enough information to begin holding them accountable for their partisan stance. What many progressives may not know is that we also have the systems in place to make "voting with your wallet" both easy and effective.

> **Myth: Companies ignore boycotts and other consumer activism.**

It's easy to be skeptical about the power of consumer activism. We've all heard about boycotts of various famous brands and maybe even participated in a few. But the brands keep showing up at our local supermarket or shopping mall. The company puts out a press release saying that it's changed its ways. The idealists who initially called for a boycott publish a counterclaim that the company is still behaving badly. It's hard for average consumers to know who's right or whether their actions have had any impact at all.

All the drama surrounding the best-publicized confrontations between companies and activists can obscure the quiet, commonplace achievements of consumer pressure. The effects are visible all around us, every day. Just consider the labels on every can, jar, and bottle on the average supermarket shelf.

The fact that our food has standardized labels at all is the result of consumers' insistence on reliable information about what we're eating and drinking. When packaged food became the norm after World War II, unscrupulous companies tried to make it hard to figure out the exact quantity inside the package. Back then, American shoppers needed "the impulses of a sleuth, the stamina of a weight-lifter, and the skill of a certified public accountant" to estimate the "unit price" and make sure they weren't getting bilked.[1] They complained loudly and persistently through groups like the Consumer Union until in 1966 the government obliged companies to stick the basic facts on every item.

Consumers' hunger for information went well beyond the basics, though. In the lifetime of the average American, all kinds of new slogans have cropped up on labels in response to consumer pressure. "Recyclable." "Dolphin Safe." "Organic." "Fair Trade." "Made Without Sweatshop Labor." "Forest Stewardship Council Certified." Some of this new label information has been mandated by the government; some of it results from big companies' adopting a voluntary code of conduct. None of it would have happened without tireless work by organized consumer advocacy groups and a throng of informed consumers demanding an ethical alternative.

Labels are a small thing. Like other signals of social responsibility, they can be abused for PR purposes. But whether or not they reflect a corporate change of heart, they are one of the most visible signs of consumer impact. They also represent the first keystone of consumer power: *information*. Any effective consumer movement must begin by informing people about the broader impact of their purchases and making them aware of alternatives.

The second keystone of consumer power is *organization*. Big companies have an advantage as long as they're dealing with scattered individuals; when consumers unite, they can suddenly find themselves a match for any company. We'll need to be well organized to make our voices heard and to pry more information out of reluctant corporations. We'll also need good organization to deal with all of the information we already have. Consumers can quickly be overwhelmed by detail; consumer advocates need to strike a balance between keeping the information simple and making sure it accurately describes a complex situation.

Fortunately, the Internet has made it dramatically easier to mobilize consumers and give them access to user-friendly information. A fresh generation of progressive organizations is taking advantage of online consumer activism to make big business a little more accountable on human rights, labor, and environmental issues. We can also use it to support and expand the Blue Sector.

Reality: The Internet has opened up new avenues for information sharing and mobilization, allowing consumers to hold companies accountable more effectively than ever before.

It used to take a lot more work to be an informed, conscientious consumer. In the Gilded Age a century ago, during the last high-water mark of corporate irresponsibility, the National Consumer League held mass public meetings in dozens of American cities to raise awareness of exploitative sweatshop labor.[2] Soon after its founding in 1982, the progressive advocacy group Co-op America began publishing *National Green Pages,* a regularly updated guide for shoppers who care about social justice and the environment. Back then, a consumer who wanted detailed information needed to seek out the meeting or buy the book. That level of effort is beyond what many people are willing to expend for the satisfaction of being an ethical consumer.

Today, the threshold is as low as clicking a mouse button. Anyone with an Internet connection can get all the consumer information he needs. Co-op America has moved *National Green Pages* online, where it's possible to search for ecofriendly companies by state and industry. The group also publishes detailed social and environmental ratings of companies online in its Responsible Shopper section.

Even with easy access to information, though, it can take a while to develop the habits of an ethical consumer. Anyone who has tried to save on paper and plastic by shopping with a reusable cloth bag has probably found out how easy it is to forget the thing at home. In the same way, it's easy to forget information about which companies are socially responsible and which are not—especially if you're an impulse buyer. Ideally, the gap between looking up consumer information and shopping should be as narrow as possible.

A groundbreaking retail Web site created in 2005, alonovo (www.alonovo.com), removes the gap entirely. Alonovo.com, whose name means "sustaining or nurturing something new" in

Latin, is a comprehensive online retailer in the style of Amazon.com, offering a wide range of products from patio furniture to DVDs to organic coffee. In addition to product and price information, it displays the name of the company that produces each item, along with the company's social and environmental ratings. So if you're buying a new kitchen blender, you can consider the labor fairness and environmental records of Braun and KitchenAid as well as the difference in price. (As of this writing, KitchenAid wins on environment, Braun on labor.)

The basic information is available at a glance, with five circles representing different progressive criteria ranked on a scale of 1 to 100. (Like us, alonovo.com gets its social responsibility data from KLD Research & Analytics, an independent analyst of corporate behavior.) Shoppers who want more detail can delve into the rankings, finding out, for example, whether a company's good environmental record is based on its ecofriendly products or its use of renewable energy. Alonovo.com users can also adjust the social responsibility criteria according to their individual values. If labor fairness is more important to you than whether a company uses a lot of recycled materials, you can weight the rankings so that alonovo.com downplays the latter and emphasizes the former. As a final sweetener, the Web site lets its users choose a nonprofit group to receive a donation with each transaction—a share of alonovo.com's "seller's fee" on Amazon.com.

As the Internet affects more and more of our shopping, tools like alonovo.com will become increasingly indispensable for progressive consumers. The online retail market mushroomed to an estimated $95 billion in 2006, but that's only the tip of the iceberg.[3] Analysts suggest that more than a quarter of all retail sales are affected by the Internet—counting everybody who compares prices and other product information online before driving out to the mall—and that by 2010 nearly *half* of all retail sales will be influenced by the Internet.[4] The more of that trade we can guide into responsible businesses, the better.

Unfortunately, alonovo.com continues the trend of separating social responsibility from political responsibility. The site has declined to rate corporations' political impact, and (perhaps inevitably, for a young online retailer) it processes its sales through Amazon.com, a red company, which gave 59 percent of its political contributions to Republicans over the last five election cycles. Politically responsible consumers may be glad to channel some of alonovo.com's profits to the League of Conservation Voters or MoveOn, but will be disappointed that Amazon also profits from every transaction.

So far there is no equivalent to alonovo.com for Americans who want to systematically integrate their political convictions into their shopping. For the first time, however, there is a one-stop source of information for progressives who want to vote with their wallets: BuyBlue.org.

Shop Where You Vote

The Democrats' loss in the 2004 presidential election was a galvanizing moment for progressives across America. For most of them, John Kerry's defeat was a spur to innovation, not an excuse for despair. In the Daily Kos online community, some progressive bloggers asked why their money should be going to the companies that had bankrolled George W. Bush so capably. It wasn't a rhetorical question. They understood that Bush's fundraising advantage was grounded in corporate support, and they intended to respond by redirecting their consumer dollars toward blue companies. As one of them pointed out, "If everybody who voted Democratic in 2004 shifted just $100 from red to blue corporations, that would represent a shift of $5 billion in the economy."[5]

Within weeks, this group of motivated strangers had organized into a nonprofit corporation and built the backbone for a new consumer information Web site called BuyBlue.org. The site is designed as a collaborative volunteer effort, much like the highly successful online encyclopedia Wikipedia. A core of long-term BuyBlue.org volunteers coordinates and verifies the work of hundreds of progressive researchers. They collect information on corporate social responsibility and political spending from dozens of obscure, potentially confusing Web sites and bring that information together in a simple, user-friendly format.

BuyBlue.org is centered on an index of America's biggest companies. Each company is assigned an icon representing its political impact. Partisan contributors are assigned either a red elephant or a blue donkey, whose size corresponds to the scale of the company's political slant. Companies that donate equally to both major parties receive a "balanced scales" icon. Companies that don't donate at all are denoted by a "no-spending" icon.

Researchers for BuyBlue.org can also attach articles on a company's behavior, which can add up to a simple positive or negative rating in several social and environmental categories. Curious BuyBlue.org users can look up the articles on which those judgments are based and judge the company's record for themselves. The real focus, however, is on informing consumers about companies' political spending. It's a simple idea, but companies immediately recognized its potential to affect their business.

BuyBlue.org launched in fall 2004, just in time for a "Blue Christmas 2004" campaign, distributing a list of progressive consumer goods companies to holiday shoppers. Though both the organization and the Blue Christmas campaign were quite small, they demonstrated the power of consumer activism to focus media and corporate attention. Within weeks, BuyBlue.org had been spotlighted by *The Washington Post,* the *San Francisco Chronicle,* FOX News, CNN, and other national and international news outlets. Raven Brooks, the chair and president of Buy-Blue.org, was taken aback by the initial impact. "Early on, I got a call on my cell phone from a number I didn't recognize. It was the chairman of Bed Bath & Beyond. I still have no idea how he got my number."

Since then, Brooks has explained the BuyBlue.org paradigm to dozens of other corporate representatives. "A decent majority of the companies who contact us are just curious. Many of them are used to the paradigm of people boycotting what they do. We prefer to highlight good behavior rather than focus on the bad, and we never use the word 'boycott.' We do encourage customers to shift where they're spending money. . . . But realistically, when we're talking about political contributions, you can't just say, 'I'm never going to deal with this industry.' Take the gas industry, where every company falls short in one way or another. So we just want customers to make their voices heard—by e-mail and phone, as well as through their spending. We provide them with the information that makes all that possible.

"Once we explain that paradigm, most companies say they can respect it and that they'd like to work with us on some level. Some companies are hostile, but that's what you'd expect, given that we draw attention to some facts they'd rather not have out there."

BuyBlue.org's volunteer cadre and its database have both grown impressively since its birth in 2004—it now has 350 researchers and entries on 500 companies. It has run annual Blue Christmas campaigns and has appealed to California car insurance customers to switch to blue providers such as Progressive, but BuyBlue.org remains most effective as an information clearinghouse rather than as a center for activism. The group's next strategic step is to localize. For many consumers, the ethical alternative to a big, irresponsible company is a smaller, environmentally sensitive local business. State and city BuyBlue.org chapters will be best placed to identify those local options. BuyBlue.org will coordinate the local groups and offer tools to help them succeed: start-up assistance, a research methodology, a place on the Web site. Whereas the core BuyBlue.org staff is engaged mostly in research and information, the local chapters will be better suited to advocacy and activism. "Boycott" might even enter their vocabulary.

Of course, conscientious consumers don't have to wait until BuyBlue.org goes local before using the Internet for activism as well as information. The new consumer information resources represented by alonovo.com and BuyBlue.org are still in their infancy, relatively speaking. They are potentially invaluable tools, but they need to attract a larger community of users before they fully come into their own. By contrast, the Internet's power to rally consumers against corporate misbehavior is already a demonstrated fact. Over the last five years, the expansion of progressive online communities (commonly known as "the netroots") has given Democrats a remarkable advantage in mobilizing their sympathizers to act.

For decades, the Republicans have used their domination of the radio dial to ratchet up pressure on companies that adopt progressive policies. Conservative talk show hosts blasted Ben & Jerry's for its founders' political stance and launched boycotts of Disney, Ford, and other companies that offer equal benefits to gay employees.[6] "Old media" such as radio are a perfect fit for the centralized conservative message machine, with one pundit pronouncing the day's talking points and keeping the ensuing discussion under close control. Right-wingers tend to use the Internet in much the same way—as a loudspeaker, an online echo chamber for the same message that goes out over the radio and FOX News.

Progressives, by contrast, are much better at using the Internet's most powerful capabilities: building independent online communities and mobilizing people for real-world activism. As we discuss later in the book, the past five years have seen the netroots come into their own as one of the dynamos driving the Democratic Party. In general, the mobilizational power of the Internet has put new vigor into progressive consumer advocacy efforts. Just ask Todd Paglia, executive director of the California-based environmental group ForestEthics.

The Customer Is Always Right

If you walked past a Victoria's Secret outlet anywhere in America on April 11, 2006, the odds are decent that you noticed a knot of protesters outside—or at least noticed their signs, which showed lingerie models aggressively brandishing chain saws. The eye-catching image was courtesy of ForestEthics, which instigated and coordinated 225 protests on that single day as part of its "Victoria's Dirty Secret" campaign.

The dirty secret, for those readers who didn't pass a protest, was that the 395 million Victoria's Secret catalogs that go out in the mail every year were being made at the expense of endangered North American forests. The great Canadian boreal forest, for example, is home to many indigenous tribes and one of the last unbroken habitats of caribou, lynx, bear, and wolves. It also provides a source of easy profit to irresponsible timber and paper companies, which prefer clear-cutting to the investment and effort required for ethical forestry. The U.S. paper industry has closed ranks against the Forestry Stewardship Council's practicable and widely praised standards for sustainable harvesting of trees. The industry's preferred alternative code of conduct is so feeble and unconvincing that it would scarcely count as a speed bump for companies racing to clear-cut the boreal forest. ForestEthics has been pressing paper companies to buck the industry consensus—to "break the logjam," executive director Todd Paglia jokes—and seek Forest Stewardship Council certification.

Like all consumer activists, ForestEthics tries to sway companies by applying the basic marketplace principle that "the customer is always right." But the customers who count, in this industry, are not individual American citizens. They are huge office supply stores like Staples and Office Depot and catalog-heavy retailers like Victoria's Secret and Williams-Sonoma. Paglia and his colleagues understand that the power of consumer activism can work all the way up the supply chain—that if enough Victoria's Secret customers demand environmentally friendly catalogs, Victoria's Secret will demand sustainable logging and milling from International Paper.

What makes ForestEthics distinctive is its skill at combining confrontation and conversation. Even while they face companies across a protest line, protesters keep up serious discussions over the conference table and offer the companies all the necessary information and resources to help them change their ways. "Back when we launched ForestEthics," explains Paglia, "on one hand, you had a bunch of large environmental organizations that worked closely with companies. On the other hand, you had a lot of small, scrappy ones (and one or two big ones like Greenpeace) that worked against companies. People said it was impossible for one organization to do both. We wanted to break that mold. . . . We're willing to work with companies, but we're not going to take no for an answer." Its uncompromising but respectful approach has earned ForestEthics the respect of its targets, and the group works hard to maintain positive relationships with individuals in the paper industry. As Paglia concisely puts it, "We try to be hard on the issues and soft on the people."

Sometimes, of course, being hard on the issues means getting hundreds of people to stand in front of an Office Depot store and wave signs to inform customers of environmental abuses. That's where the mobilizing power of the Internet comes in. Paglia describes how their campaigns have changed since ForestEthics first challenged Staples in 2000: "Ten years ago, if you were able to get fifteen protests on one day, that would be an incredible thing. You had to slog through and find enough people around the state or country who were interested, who cared about the issue and were willing to go out and do something. Now flash forward to the present: we can get 250 protests on one day."

Part of the difference, in Paglia's judgment, is that more Americans have become aware of the disproportionate power of big corporations and are willing to protest against it. Part of the difference is simply having a Web site linked to a growing world of online activism. "Take the Victoria's Secret campaign. We have been getting 50,000 to 100,000 unique visitors every month to the campaign Web page. When we put out a notice on the Web page . . . just getting a response from one or two percent gives you a huge event."

Ultimately, ForestEthics' most impressive achievement during the Victoria's Secret campaign was not launching more than 750 protests over a two-year time span, but the partnership it quietly built with the company behind the scenes. Paglia and his colleagues refused to compromise on the issues but never stopped engaging with Victoria's Secret's management. Their reasonable suggestions eventually fell on receptive ears. The protest-weary company agreed to press its main paper supplier to have four mills certified by the Forest Stewardship Council. Victoria's Secret also agreed to phase out of endangered forests, to establish and play a leadership role in a catalog environmental council, and to put $1 million into endangered-forest research programs. Meanwhile, ForestEthics has built a relationship with other catalog retailers such as Williams-Sonoma, which are now demanding that their mills get FSC certification. The logjam is breaking.

ForestEthics' success shows that intelligent consumer action can have a huge impact, especially when it's combined with the organizing capacity of the Internet. But Paglia doesn't claim that his group is "particularly techno-savvy." Its Internet mobilizing efforts have focused primarily on its own Web site, not on linking to bigger online communities. The promising exception is ForestEthics' recently launched partnership with Care2, the largest online community portal, which has about 6 million members. When Care2's front page featured ForestEthics' campaign to protect the Great Bear Rainforest in Canada, community members responded with 10,000 faxes and e-mails to the British Columbian government. "British Columbia cares about tourism dollars," Paglia explained. "And if you look at the membership of Care2, it's about 72 percent women, who tend to be well off in relative terms"—just the kind of potential tourist who can command attention in the Canadian province.

All in all, Paglia cheerfully admits, when it comes to making full use of the netroots, "we're still pretty scrappy. If we invest more on the Internet side and use more of the techniques that MoveOn and the Dean campaign pioneered, I think we'll see an even steeper trend [of increased participation]. I don't think it's close to maxed out yet."

When the Netroots Come Marching In

The netroots unquestionably played the lead role in mustering consumer and shareholder action against the archconservative Sinclair Broadcast Group in 2004. Sinclair is the largest independent owner of television stations in America; it currently owns, operates, or services fifty-eight television stations around the nation. It also has the distinction of being the media outlet farthest out on the red end of the spectrum—a distinction that has repeatedly translated into behavior that has been both intensely partisan and bad for business.

Over the last five election cycles, Sinclair's top three executives and corporate PAC have made $117,850 in political contributions, of which 95 percent went to Republicans and a mere 5 percent to Democrats. The company has actually become more partisan over time; in 2004 and 2006, Sinclair's corporate PAC gave 100 percent of its contributions to Republicans. By comparison, FOX News looks positively fair and balanced—the top executives of media giant News Corporation, which owns FOX Broadcasting Company, gave only $95,994 over the same period, with 24 percent going to Democrats and 76 percent to Republicans. Even the conservative radio conglomerate Clear Channel Communications was less slanted, giving 35 percent of its total $877,300 to Democrats and 65 percent to Republicans.[7]

Some red companies donate to the Republicans out of a misguided belief that it's good for profits; others donate because they are ideological bedfellows with the most socially irresponsible GOP strategists. Sinclair is an enthusiastic member of the latter category. Its most distinctive and enduring piece of original programming was "The Point," a two-minute segment in which corporate vice president Mark Hyman ranted about the damage that liberals, Democrats, and the French were doing to America. Until dropping "The Point" just before the most recent national elections in November 2006, Sinclair required all of its stations to run the segment during their news programming and refused to let them label it as editorial or commentary.[8]

Not surprisingly, Sinclair has repeatedly stumbled into scandal over the last few years for bringing partisanship to the public airwaves. When the conservative pundit Armstrong Williams was illegally paid $240,000 in government money to offer "favorable commentaries" on Bush's education policy, he found an open door for his propaganda at Sinclair.[9] In addition to using his regular spots on the company's "News Central" to praise Bush's policy, Williams convinced Sinclair to broadcast a reverential interview with Education Secretary Rod Paige. The disgusted Sinclair producer who had to edit Williams's interview called it "the worst piece of TV I've ever been associated with. . . . In retrospect, it was so clearly propaganda."[10] Williams never disclosed that the government was paying him for his rapturous support of its policies, and the nonpartisan Government Accountability Office eventually found that this put Williams and the U.S. Department of Education in violation of federal laws prohibiting covert propaganda.[11]

Of all Sinclair's controversies, however, the *Stolen Honor* scandal in 2004 was the most telling. It powerfully illustrated two facts: that the company's partisanship was terrible for business and that progressive consumer and shareholder activism can make a powerful difference even at a right-wing ideological stalwart like Sinclair.

During the final stages of the close-fought 2004 presidential election, Sinclair declared that all of its TV stations (62 at the time, which together reached roughly a quarter of the American population)[12] would be obliged to show an hour-long program called "Stolen Honor: Wounds That Never Heal." The program was labeled a documentary, but critics from former FCC Chairman Reed Hundt to Sinclair Broadcasting's own Washington bureau chief, Jon Leiberman, recognized that it was in essence an extended attack ad against Democratic candidate John Kerry.[13] The program featured many of the same Vietnam veterans, false allegations, and misleading innuendoes that had driven the earlier "Swift Boat" campaign to smear Kerry's military record. Whereas the Swift Boat gang had put their anti-Kerry screeds across in a series of explicitly political ads, "Stolen Honor" (like Armstrong Williams's paid interviews and Mark Hyman's rants) was trying to masquerade as news.

The biased program immediately drew fierce criticism, but Sinclair was prepared to dig in its heels. The company fired Bureau Chief Leiberman (himself a self-identified two-time Bush voter) for publicly voicing his qualms about the "documentary." Thanks to the netroots, however, progressive outrage was quickly channeled into consumer activism targeting Sinclair's advertisers. Blogs like Daily Kos and Talking Points Memo pointed their readership to a full list of advertisers, which included companies like Procter & Gamble, Circuit City, and Toyota. Thousands of progressive consumers began contacting those companies to make their displeasure known. Sinclair's stock price promptly plummeted by 17 percent, representing a $105 million loss for its shareholders.[14] The shareholders threatened to sue, and the company clumsily retreated. Sinclair ended up airing a disjointed program about the controversy that cobbled together clips from "Stolen Honor" with pro-Kerry footage and questions about President Bush's own record in Vietnam—a far cry from its original full-throated propaganda.

These netroots examples confirm that every progressive can make a difference through consumer activism, even to corporations that may think they can ignore individual consumers. We may not buy anything directly from an irresponsible logging company, but we have power over it as customers of Home Depot or OfficeMax. A media giant may not care if we stop watching its shows, but it will certainly care if we stir up a hornet's nest among its advertisers. The Internet has made it easier for us to find a point of leverage and mobilize enough ordinary people to make a change.

A fast-growing number of business leaders and conscientious consumers worldwide are finding ways to combine doing good with making a profit. For example, despite the name, the "(PRODUCT) RED" campaign, whose most famous advocate is the singer-activist Bono. The campaign is harnessing Western consumer spending to counter the African AIDS epidemic. Every company involved (including Blue Sector members Apple and Gap Inc.) has created a special line of RED products and has committed a percentage of every RED purchase to the Global Fund's fight against AIDS in Africa.[15] The goal is to create a long-term, sustainable flow of private capital to the Global Fund. By the beginning of 2007, the campaign had raised more than $20 million for the fund and disbursed $10.25 million to HIV/AIDS programs in Rwanda and Swaziland. Meanwhile, the participating companies were reporting an enthusiastic consumer response. Dan Henkle, the Gap Inc. vice president for social responsibility, told us that not only had the Gap found it hard to keep its special RED line in stock, but it had been selling out of red-colored clothing that had nothing to do with the campaign. Similarly, according to Apple vice president Greg Joswiak, "Customer response to the iPod nano RED Special Edition has been off the charts."[16]

Just imagine what could happen if we consciously applied the same sort of consumer power to strengthening the Blue Sector. Before your next trip to the mall, check on BuyBlue.org to see where your favorite consumer companies are sending your money. Learn what alternatives you have. E-mail companies to let them know what you think of their political as well as social behavior. Let your consumer dollar shore up your vote, not work against it.

Who Are You Calling a Consumer?

We can't end this chapter without a word of dissent from Reverend Billy. Any of our readers who have encountered the reverend and his Church of Stop Shopping are unlikely to have forgotten the experience. The tall, white-suited Reverend Billy has a blond pompadour and the diction of a street preacher. He hops up and down while exorcising demons of consumerism from cash registers around the world, punctuating his message with loud shouts of "Changellujah!" and imploring distracted shoppers to "be saved from the Shopocalypse!" His Stop Shopping Gospel Choir, thirty enthusiastic volunteers with terrific voices, is usually somewhere nearby belting out the church's theme: "Stop shopping, start living!"

Reverend Billy is the alter ego of performance artist Bill Talen, a New Yorker who invented the character in the late 1990s to protest against the mass-market reinvention of Times Square.[17] Talen is probably the most entertaining face of the anti-consumerism movement, and his Church of Stop Shopping is political theater at its finest. Their basic message is simple: we Americans spend too much time and money shopping for things we don't need. Big corporations are trying to turn every corner of life into a branded product. We need to resist being defined simply as "consumers" and look at the social and environmental consequences of our consumption. We need to protect unique community space and local businesses from being overwhelmed by homogeneous corporate franchises and brands.

The reverend is a charming but uncompromising man, with no time for protestations of corporate virtue. His favorite targets include a number of blue companies, and he would prefer a quirky local shop to even the most socially and environmentally responsible chain store. He dismisses the (PRODUCT) RED campaign as a mistake, an attempt to harness consumerism when we should be reining it in (while the choir sings, "Can We Shop enough To Save Africa?").

We mention him because we recognize that the anticon-sumerism movement gets a lot of things right. People are more than just consumers, and in a world increasingly saturated with advertising it can be easy to lose track of that fact. Small local businesses are often the heart and soul of a neighborhood yet find it hard to compete with big national chains. The space around us is becoming ever more cluttered with advertising. Most of us could stand to shop less and save more, to question whether we really need a pricey entertainment system or new car. And no, we can't shop enough to save Africa—though $20 million in less than a year is nothing to sniff at.

When we call for consumer activism, we don't want people to go out and consume more, just as we didn't design the Blue Index to draw more money into politics. In both cases, though, we need to work within the imperfect realities of the American economy. We're not going to see a revolution against consumerism any time soon. For the foreseeable future, most Americans will continue to buy plenty of goods and services from big companies, because the companies offer real advantages in consistency, familiarity, and price. Since in the short term we aren't going to stem the massive flow of consumer spending, it's crucial that we channel it in the right direction— toward those companies that have figured out how to succeed financially while being socially and politically responsible.

Meanwhile, to the extent that we do shop less and save more, we'll be creating wealth that needs to be invested wisely over the long haul. In our next chapter, we look at ways for progressive shareholders to put their investment money and their proxy votes to work for the Blue Sector.

CHAPTER 7

Painting Wall Street Blue

Politically Responsible Shareholder Activism

CONSUMER SPENDING MAY BE THE MEAT AND DRINK
of corporate America, but investor dollars are its lifeblood. High
market capitalization is a compelling sign of a company's health
and vigor; an anemic share price leaves the company vulnerable
to being snapped up by a competitor. Not surprisingly, business
executives pay close attention to anything that might frighten
shareholders away. Frame a problem purely in terms of social
responsibility, and most corporations do their best to ignore you;
frame it in terms of shareholder value, and you have the boardroom's ear. If we're going to fix corporate America's partisan
slant, progressive shareholder activists must challenge Wall
Street's complacency about the risks and rewards of ideological
political spending.

You don't have to be rich to be an investor, nor do you even
have to pay attention to the stock market. Plenty of people who
prefer baseball stats to stock prices and toss out the "Finance"
section of the newspaper unread are shareowners without real-

izing it. If you have a 401(k), you're an investor, even if you've hardly paid attention to it since you were hired. If you have a pension through your job, you're probably an investor—especially if you're a teacher or other public employee, or if you belong to a union. Big pension funds like CalPERS and CalSTRS (the California funds for public employees and teachers, respectively) are among the most activist and influential investors in the American stock market today. Many churches, synagogues, and universities also have a good-sized endowment invested partly in stocks. One way or another, you or an institution you belong to can probably reinforce the Blue Sector through shareholder activism.

Although shareholders are the owners of corporate America, it's harder than you'd expect for them to hold corporate executives accountable. In theory, they steer the companies they own through a form of indirect democracy: the shareholders elect the board of directors, who then choose the company's executives and monitor their performance. In practice, thanks to the current rules of the U.S. Securities and Exchange Commission (SEC) which regulates publicly traded companies, a company's executives are usually able to influence or control who gets nominated as a director. The slate of directors is put to a symbolic vote at the company's annual meeting, where shareholders can only vote yes or abstain. As one shareholder advocate, Robert Monks, recently put it, "The American shareholder cannot nominate directors, he cannot remove them, he cannot—except at the arbitrary pleasure of the SEC—communicate advice to them. Democracy is a cruelly misleading word to describe the situation of the American shareholder in 2006."[1]

In the absence of democratic control over the board or management, shareholders must resort to other methods to influence the companies they own. The bluntest and simplest tool at investors' disposal is, of course, the power to sell the stock of companies that are headed in the wrong direction. Investors who go beyond that and attempt to actively engage with corporate management are generally referred to as activist shareholders. Much of their engagement centers on proposing resolutions for a vote at the annual meeting.

When a 15 Percent Vote Is a Win

A shareholder resolution is simply a request that the managers or board of a company take action on some issue. Any investors who own sufficient stock can propose one. Most resolutions have to do with corporate governance, such as challenging excessive CEO pay and severance packages or requesting that the company nominate more independent directors to its board. Many also have to do with social or environmental responsibility, such as requesting that the company adopt a nondiscrimination policy on employee sexual orientation or that the company find ways to reduce its exposure to climate change risk. Assuming the shareholder resolution meets various SEC guidelines, it will be published in the company's proxy statement and voted on by all shareholders at the annual meeting.

These resolutions may seem futile at first glance. They are not legally binding, and they almost never win a majority of votes, especially if they're opposed by management. Corporate executives and incumbent board members usually own large blocks of shares themselves. Many institutional investors have a "never vote against management" policy—especially large mutual funds, which hope that companies will channel employee retirement accounts, pension fund money, and other lucrative contracts their way.[2] Many other investors can't be bothered to vote at all, effectively handing their votes to management.

Despite all these handicaps, however, shareholder resolutions are a potent tool for affecting corporate behavior. Corporate executives know how solidly the deck is stacked against critical resolutions; they understand that even a seemingly unimpressive 10 percent vote can reflect broad concerns or strong convictions among their shareholder base. Resolutions also draw attention to issues that managers would rather ignore, especially if the resolutions win enough support to stay on the ballot year after year. (Per SEC rules, if a resolution wins at least 3 percent of the vote in its first year, at least 6 percent in its second year, and at least 10 percent thereafter, it can be submitted to the shareholders again and again.) A sustained campaign of shareholder activism can seriously affect the company's reputation on Wall Street and in the international press. As a result, though a company's managers are not required by law or landslide votes to acquiesce to shareholder resolutions, they often do.

This explains one of the more counterintuitive principles of shareholder advocacy: a withdrawn resolution is a win. In the 2005 proxy season, activist investors filed thirty-five resolutions on climate change, calling on companies to adopt a responsible policy to deal with greenhouse gas emissions. At seventeen of those companies, the resolutions were withdrawn before the annual meeting because the company chose to negotiate an acceptable compromise and avoid the publicity and hassle of a shareholder campaign. Half of the resolutions thus accomplished their purpose without ever coming to a vote.[3]

Resolutions that do make it to the annual meeting are getting an increasingly positive response, as investors realize that their votes send a critical signal to corporations. "More and more, shareholders are voting in favor of resolutions," says Steven Schueth, president of First Affirmative Financial Network, a financial advisory firm that specializes in socially responsible investment. "Five to seven years ago, we'd win 3 percent or 4 percent of the vote and we'd be thrilled. But we're seeing an uptick every year, so that now they win maybe 15 percent to 20 percent of the vote. That's a lot of investors, and it's often enough to lead the management to change."[4] The 2006 proxy season was the most successful ever for social and environmental resolutions; more than a quarter of the proposals that came to a shareholder vote broke the 15 percent support threshold.[5]

One reason for the current popularity of shareholder activism is the steadily accumulating evidence that it's good for business. Two Harvard Business School scholars found that in companies that went through a proxy contest between shareholders and management, shareholders on average enjoyed an 8 percent higher long-term return—no matter what the outcome of the contest.[6] The substance of the resolution mattered less than its unspoken message: that shareholders were monitoring executives and were willing to hold them accountable. In another well-known study, researchers looked at eight years of *Wall Street Journal* records and identified 144 firms whose shareholders had actively engaged with management over various issues (mostly involving corporate governance). In the three years following a shareholder intervention, the firms' shares performed on average 23 percent better than expected.[7] The researchers suggested that executives simply tend to behave more responsibly when they know they are being watched.

A raft of studies has focused on CalPERS, the California state employee pension fund, since it became a driving force in American shareholder advocacy in the late 1980s. CalPERS publishes an annual list of "targeted" companies in its portfolio whose corporate governance, social policy, or stock market performance it considers unsatisfactory. It then does its best to transform those companies through dialogue with management, press releases, resolutions, and other forms of shareholder activism. The majority of analysts have found that CalPERS's engagement has added substantial stock market value to targeted firms—and that its visible, aggressive advocacy has been more effective than its quieter, behind-the-scenes advocacy.[8] A recent study of "the CalPERS effect" by investment analysts at Wilshire Associates concluded that American investors waste a great deal of time and energy trying to exploit small price discrepancies in a largely efficient stock market when there are higher returns to be made by identifying badly managed firms and setting them right through CalPERS-style shareholder activism.[9]

Cracking Open Cracker Barrel

Shareholder activism can help not only in making companies better governed and more profitable but also in making them more just. Just consider the shareholders' movement to protect gay employees from corporate discrimination. Fifteen years ago, the SEC wouldn't allow investors to challenge executives' bigotry through shareholder resolutions, but after a long fight in the marketplace, court, and boardroom, activists have successfully won over both the SEC and the great majority of large American corporations.

Back in 1991, and continuing until 2002, in one of the most blatant acts of antigay intolerance by a major American corporation, the Cracker Barrel restaurant chain (a 92 percent red company) declared that all its employees were expected to "demonstrate normal heterosexual values" and fired 11 lesbian and gay workers.[10] This outrage drew immediate fire from civil rights groups, of course. It also upset institutional shareholders, who feared the damage that an overtly discriminatory employment policy would do to the company's reputation—not to mention the damage that the accompanying protests and boycotts would do to the value of their shares. A New York City pension fund swiftly submitted a shareholder proposal calling on Cracker Barrel to reverse its policy and adopt an antidiscrimination clause.

Cracker Barrel flat-out refused to include the resolution in its annual proxy statement. As a general rule, companies can leave out any shareholder proposal that "deals with a matter relating to the conduct of . . . ordinary business operations."[11] The SEC initially upheld Cracker Barrel's argument that "a company's employment policies and practices" for rank-and-file workers were part of its ordinary business operations, not a matter of shareholder interest. According to this ruling, shareholders could intervene on executive-level employment issues but must leave "general workforce" policies to management's discretion.[12]

Needless to say, as owners of Cracker Barrel, the company's shareholders considered themselves both morally and financially interested in a policy of open discrimination against gay employees. They didn't want to micromanage the company's employment practices (the real point of the "ordinary business" exclusion), but they were determined to challenge a sweeping rule that put their company on the wrong side of a major social issue. There's inevitably a blurry middle area between day-to-day business practices where management should be given free rein and broad policy issues suitable for shareholder intervention. By drawing a clear line around general workforce employment policies and blocking all shareholder resolutions on the subject, the SEC mistakenly took too much voice away from a company's owners.

After seven years of determined pressure from shareholder advocates and a 1996 congressional request to review the ruling, the SEC finally caved in. Its 1998 amendments to its ruling reversed the Cracker Barrel decision, allowing shareholders to file resolutions that affected general employees if the proposal raised "sufficiently significant social policy issues." [13] Conscientious investors promptly redoubled their campaign to convince Cracker Barrel's management that discriminating against gay and lesbian employees was both unjust and bad for business.

That shareholder campaign ultimately had a dramatic impact on company policy and the overall culture of corporate America. In 1996, only the slimmest majority of Fortune 500 companies—251, to be exact—included the term "sexual orientation" in their antidiscrimination statements, and just 19 offered benefits to same-sex domestic partners. By 2006, thanks to constant shareholder pressure, 430 Fortune 500 companies explicitly protected gay employees in their antidiscrimination policies, and 254 companies offered domestic partner benefits. [14] Not even Cracker Barrel could withstand the tidal wave of investor opinion. In November 2002, after a nondiscrimination resolution won proxy support from 58 percent of its shareholders, Cracker Barrel's board voted unanimously to add "sexual orientation" to its antidiscrimination policy statement. [15]

Today we are calling on all progressive investors to capitalize on their power as shareholders and to challenge managers who promote an ethically irresponsible, financially short-term, or politically unjust vision. If your money is invested by a mutual fund or investment adviser, that fund or adviser is entitled to vote on your behalf on all resolutions. Since August 2004, it is also legally required to tell you how it has voted and explain its voting guidelines. Find out how it has been using your vote, and let it know what you think of its record. If your university, union, church, or synagogue is an investor, ask for its voting history on shareholder resolutions. If you control your own investments, be diligent about voting when the annual proxy statement shows up in your mailbox. An active, responsible shareholder base is the best guarantee that blue companies will continue to act blue.

As we've said throughout the book, Blue Sector companies are hardly above criticism. In our own index, we drop any company that gets three strikes on KLD's social responsibility ratings, but shareholder advocacy is a powerful tool for turning one- or two-strike blue companies into paragons of social responsibility. The Gap's candid reporting on its labor standards was motivated not only by critical scrutiny from antisweatshop advocacy groups but also by pressure from socially responsible investors such as Domini, Calvert, and the As You Sow Foundation.[16] Shareholder resolutions also provide a forum to hold companies accountable for promised reforms. All progressive shareholders should be sure to read through each year's proposals and vote according to their values.

What about red companies? Up to this point in the book, we've been advocating the bluntest method for shareholders to send a message: don't buy red company shares. The partisan slant of the current S&P 500 is anything but subtle; we would argue that now is the time for prompt, unsubtle ways of restoring balance to corporate America. Investing exclusively in the Blue Sector is the single best way to ensure that your money supports your progressive values, politically as well as socially.

True, by not investing in red companies, you give up the chance to engage them from the inside, but many corporate leaders are too deeply invested in the myths we've been debunking to be reasoned out of them. Nothing will snap them out of their trance faster or more effectively than a crowd of progressive shareholders heading for the exits.

Still, progressives who choose to maintain their investments in red companies have some resources available to challenge the companies' political bias. Like most other forms of blue activism, this will fly in the face of the widespread reluctance (even by progressive shareholder advocates) to challenge a corporation's involvement in politics. "Government affairs" have traditionally been considered a normal management responsibility, the sort of thing that shareholders should leave to CEOs. As a result, corporate executives enjoy remarkably little accountability in their use of company funds for political ends. They are legally required to report their PAC contributions to federal candidates, but it's rare that any shareholder questions the business rationale behind even this visible political spending. Then there's the invisible money—the multibillion-dollar corporate aquifer feeding nonprofit political groups, lobbying organizations, and politicized trade associations. None of this money needs to be explicitly reported, let alone justified. Partisan CEOs have so far operated on the assumption that American shareholders aren't paying attention. It's time to change their minds.

**Myth: Smart shareholders don't
interfere with a company's
"government affairs" decisions.**

Much of the drama in HBO's acclaimed series *The Sopranos* centers around the flimsy wall that separates Tony Soprano's Mafia family from his nuclear family. Tony's wife and kids know how he makes his money, but by unspoken agreement, they don't look too closely at Tony's job or ask the wrong sorts of questions. Until very recently, most investors have had a similar approach to corporate lobbying expenditures and other political contributions. They recognize that companies are paying for access to politicians, which can result in highly profitable legislative or regulatory decisions.

As a result, they tend to shy away from demanding explicit, transparent accounting of political spending at the companies they own. When an uncommonly bold shareholder does inquire what benefit a company gets from its political donations, company bosses generally deflect the question with bland language about the importance of "supporting the electoral process" and "participation in the legislative/regulatory process."[17] This thinly conceals the same sort of incredulity expressed by Tony Soprano: "I have to spell this out for you?"

Of course, not all corporate political spending is inherently shady. As any environmental or consumer rights advocate will tell you, it takes money just to make an honest political case—to hire an expert staff, travel to Washington, research and publish advocacy materials and disseminate them on Capitol Hill, stay on top of press coverage, and so on. Business leaders have an honest case to make in Washington on issues that affect their industries. They also have the right to fund political advocacy groups that promote a particular vision for the American economy and government. Unless their political spending is transparent, however, we have no way to know when it has descended to the level of bribery—and shareholders have no way to judge whether it is a genuinely profitable use of their investment dollars.

The Jack Abramoff circus should have destroyed any illusion that corporations, lobbyists, and politicians can be trusted to draw the line between honest advocacy and bribery. The full extent of Congress's corruption at the height of Republican control remains astonishing. Under the guise of fact-finding missions or charity fund-raisers, corporations handed out free junkets to legislators. A recent Center for Public Integrity report found that between January 2000 and June 2005, "members of Congress and their aides took at least 23,000 trips—valued at almost $50 million—financed by private sponsors, many of them corporations, trade associations and nonprofit groups with business on Capitol Hill."[18] These included "at least 200 trips to Paris, 150 to Hawaii and 140 to Italy," those well-known "fact-finding" hot spots. Without any real excuse to veil their bribes, lobbyists showered members of Congress with gifts and perquisites such as skybox seats at NCAA tournament games, luxury hotel stays, and complimentary meals at swanky Washington restaurants. This shows the real consequences of keeping political money in the shadows.

Transparency is the single most important factor in keeping business and government honest. Corruption is like a mold on our political system; we can go a long way toward killing it off with nothing more than sunlight and air. Some politicians, of course, are beyond embarrassment. Think of former Republican Majority Leader Tom DeLay, who had accepted so many gifts and favors from big corporate donors over the years that he didn't see any irony in letting the tobacco giant R. J. Reynolds provide him with a corporate jet flight to his own arraignment for unethical campaign fund-raising.[19] Even after the Abramoff scandal broke, the GOP legislative bosses couldn't bring themselves to alter the rules about taking "gifts" from lobbyists. But the end of that story demonstrates the political benefits of transparency: when lawmakers themselves lose their shame, American voters have the information they need to throw the bums out, as they did with the hopelessly tainted Republican Congress in November 2006. In the same way, transparency gives shareholders the facts they need to challenge indefensibly partisan executives.

Some investors will still be tempted to avert their eyes from less than transparent political spending for profits' sake. Corporate executives are quick to offer anecdotes about the legal and regulatory benefits their political spending has brought—for example, they might observe that a $500,000 investment in lobbying Congress produced a policy decision that saved a company $5 million. Even if we set aside moral issues, unless a company's board and shareholders can review all political expenditures by management, they have no way of knowing whether political contributions are aiding the bottom line. The weak stock market performance of red S&P 500 companies over the last five years ought to dent investors' complacency about the rewards of political contributions.

The good news is that more and more investors are waking up to the scale of the problem. They recognize that secret expenditures without internal controls are bad news for shareholders. Since 2004, a growing shareholder movement has been calling for transparency and accountability in political spending.

> **Reality: Political spending is an issue of shareholder value and should be of concern to every investor.**

If we asked you to guess the number one issue raised recently in socially responsible shareholder resolutions, you might guess climate change or sweatshop labor. In fact, the largest number of resolutions demanded that companies fully disclose their political contributions. Fifty-one resolutions were proposed on the subject in 2004, forty-two in 2005, and twenty-nine in 2006, far above the number of resolutions on any other single social issue.[20] Levels of shareholder support for these proposals have risen steadily. Last year, the twenty-nine resolutions that came to a vote received on average 21.89 percent approval, which, given the many built-in limitations on shareholder voting, represents a resounding endorsement.[21]

This surge in political shareholder activism is thanks mainly to the Center for Political Accountability (CPA), a nonpartisan advocacy group founded in 2003. The organization's activities are based on a simple idea: corporate executives ought to have a business rationale for their political spending, and they should be willing to explain that rationale to the owners of the company. As codirector John Richardson explains, "Our focus is on making companies more transparent with their political giving. . . . This is an issue mainstream investors are concerned about. It gets to the core of good corporate governance practice and shareholder value."

Beginning in the 2004 proxy season, the CPA organized and piloted a coalition of institutional investors to call for full disclosure of companies' political contributions. The resolutions sponsored by these shareholders (mainly union pension funds and religious groups) aimed to bring two crucial values back into corporate political spending: accountability and transparency.

To make real accountability possible, companies have to set explicit principles and procedures for investing company money in politics. Who decides on the amount to be contributed? Who approves and monitors contributions? How does a contribution tie in to the company's business strategy, and how can the company measure its success? Given the seven-figure scale of annual political expenditures at many big firms, it's remarkable how few are willing to explain to shareholders their guidelines for investing in politics. In a February 2005 report, the CPA analyzed 120 large-cap corporations for their political accountability. It found that while 89 of the companies had posted a general contribution policy on their Web sites for shareholder review, only two companies disclosed specific criteria for their political spending.[22]

Even more disturbing for shareholders, few companies have adequate internal structures of approval and oversight to hold managers accountable for their political spending. Just 50 companies (less than half the total) said they required prior approval of political contributions by shareholders or the board. Eight companies claimed to have executive-level oversight of political contributions. The board of directors, in theory the instrument by which shareholders can guide the company in the right direction, was almost universally left in the dark. Despite the board's legal "duty of care" to oversee business strategies that can have a major financial impact, only three companies claimed to have board-level oversight of political contributions.[23]

Contribution Camouflage

If companies performed badly on accountability, their transparency record was truly dismal. In 2005 only two companies (Morgan Stanley and Pfizer) made public reports on the full amount of their political contributions.[24] At every other big

American corporation, shareholders who wanted to understand the company's full political impact (and risk exposure) would have had to hunt down disclosure statements from dozens of different sources—and resort to guesswork in a few areas where corporate political spending can still be effectively invisible.

On the national level, shareholders would need to consult the company PAC filings with the Federal Election Commission (FEC) for contributions to federal candidates, political parties, and committees. On the state level, they would need to hunt down disclosure reports state by state. To identify contributions to political advocacy groups (commonly known as "527 groups," from the section of the tax code that governs their operations), shareholders would need to scan the IRS database of 527 group filings. To find out how much a given company spends on lobbying, shareholders would need to look up lobbyists' filings with the clerk of the House, the secretary of the Senate, and fifty state legislatures with wildly varying disclosure rules. There are a few Web sites that do their best to collate some of this data and make it publicly available, most notably PoliticalMoneyLine, the Center for Responsive Politics, the Center for Public Integrity, and the National Institute on Money in State Politics. Despite heroic efforts, they can produce inaccurate or contradictory results when trying to keep on top of filings from thousands of PACs, 527 groups, and lobbyists.

On top of all that, for the time being, one category of corporate political spending remains invisible: the millions of dollars channeled through nonprofit trade associations such as the U.S. Chamber of Commerce, the Business Roundtable, and the American Tort Reform Association. In what essentially amounts to political money laundering, companies can make unlimited contributions to these associations, which are then free to put that money behind various candidates and issues without identifying their corporate donors. In the words of the Center for Political Accountability, "Trade associations have become the Swiss banks of American politics.[25]

Trade associations are one type of nonprofit 501(c) groups (again named after a clause in the tax code), which, unlike 527 groups, are presumed to have a primary mission other than political advocacy. Accordingly, 501(c) groups don't have the same financial disclosure responsibilities as 527s; their expenditures and donors don't have to be reported in any clear, comprehensive breakdown. In return, they are supposed to limit their election-related activities, focusing their political resources on voter education and issue advocacy. Any money they spend advocating for a candidate is taxable and must be declared, and if they spend too much on campaigning, they could in theory be penalized and lose their tax status. The IRS has never spent much effort on auditing trade associations, however. Many 501(c) groups have consequently become conduits for undeclared political spending, especially since the 2002 McCain-Feingold campaign finance law closed off other avenues for corporate soft money.

The U.S. Chamber of Commerce and its subsidiary, the Institute for Legal Reform, have practically reinvented themselves for this purpose. In a September 11, 2001, story that was largely overlooked because of the events of that day, *Wall Street Journal* reporters found that the U.S. Chamber had "created several special accounts to take in money for projects on behalf of individual companies or groups of companies."[26] What kinds of projects? For the most part, red companies such as Wal-Mart, Home Depot, and Qwest Communications International wanted to invisibly influence key legislative or judicial elections. As a 501(c) organization, the *Journal* explained, the U.S. Chamber "isn't required to report the sources of its funding, which makes it an attractive vehicle for those . . . who sometimes like to operate under the radar." Nine months before the McCain-Feingold bill became law, a U.S. Chamber political adviser predicted, "We'll start having political shops inside the business groups. They will be full-service combat shops. I think you will ultimately see more soft money in ways that are more difficult to trace." [27]

This hard-to-trace soft money has since played a decisive role in many elections. For example, when, in 2004, a consumer advocate, Deborah Senn, was running in the Democratic primaries for attorney general of Washington state, she suddenly found herself the subject of a $1.4 million attack ad. The ad, which cost more than the total combined broadcasting budget of Senn and her three competitors, was sponsored by the opaquely named Voter Education Committee. The Washington State Public Disclosure Commission investigated this exorbitant expenditure, and (after weeks of legal pressure) discovered that the sole funder of the attack ad on Senn was actually the U.S. Chamber of Commerce. Senn ultimately lost the election to her Republican rival, in large part due to the unexpectedly expensive and damaging primary campaign. [28]

501(c) status should not be a guarantee of invisibility; legally, trade associations are required to disclose their political spending to the IRS and pay income taxes on it. In practice, most have been reluctant to acknowledge any of their spending as political. The watchdog group Public Citizen recently alerted the IRS to the remarkable inconsistency between the U.S. Chamber of Commerce's triumphant boasts of influence ("the Chamber invested up to $30 million in the November 2nd [2004] elections") and its declared political expenditures to the IRS (none at all for 2000–2002, and a startlingly low $14 million for 2004). [29]

Despite all the obscure channels through which corporate money can flow to politics, companies continue to claim that shareholders can turn to "publicly available" reports to get all the relevant information. Richardson and his colleagues at the CPA are asking companies to cut through the fog and provide a clear, semiannual report of all political spending. For each contribution, the company should be able to identify the decision makers and explain how their decision was justified in terms of the company's political contributions policy.

Good for Shareholders, Good for Progressives

Whether or not they're progressive, smart shareholders ought to pay close attention to corporate political spending for two key reasons. First, as documented in the CPA's report *The Green Canary,* high levels of political contributions can be "a canary in the mine shaft"—an early warning sign associated with unsavory business practices. Companies that contribute significantly more than the average for their industry may be trying to buy political cover for a highly risky or dishonest approach to business. Of the big companies that were entangled in the 2001–2002 wave of corporate scandals, "Enron, Global Crossing, WorldCom, Qwest and Westar Energy each made corporate contributions a key part of their business strategies, enabling them to avoid oversight, engage in alleged illegal activities and gain uncharacteristic advantage in the marketplace—the combination of which led to their ignominious downfall at the expense of their shareholders."[30] How expensive? The CPA estimates that those five companies alone took more than $285 billion in shareholder money down with them.[31]

The second major shareholder risk is damage to a company's

reputation. A corporation with inadequate controls on political contributions and lobbying is more likely to have its good name tarnished by the ethical lapses of a rogue executive. Consider the 2003 lobbying scandal at Boeing, which *BusinessWeek* tersely attributed to "Flawed strategy. Lax controls. A weak board."[32] For years Boeing's board (and shareholders) did not adequately challenge CEO Phil Condit's "ethical lapses and managerial blunders," leading to a culture of excess and impunity among the top executives.[33] Ultimately, in the midst of a million-dollar lobbying campaign to convince the air force to lease Boeing planes, Boeing's chief financial officer illegally arranged a lucrative job for the procurement officer who was handling the deal from the government side.[34] The scandal brought down Condit, lost Boeing the $18 billion air force contract, earned it the suspicion of its largest customers, and (after three years of government investigation) cost the company a $615 million fine. If Boeing's board had been closely monitoring the company's lobbying and political behavior, it might have demanded a change in the executive culture before the company's reputation was blemished by corruption.

Setting aside the obvious stigma of being caught making a bribe, all political spending carries a message. Recall the 1991 Cracker Barrel case, where investors were rightly alarmed that their company had declared itself antigay. Today, even though most big companies include sexual orientation in their nondiscrimination policies, many still send the same message as Cracker Barrel by contributing money to antigay groups and candidates. Consider, for example, the political action committee Americans for a Republican Majority (ARMPAC), which collected funds from S&P 500 companies such as SBC Communications (now AT&T), BellSouth, Altria Group, and Union Pacific and then disseminated the money to antigay activist organizations such as the Traditional Values Coalition.[35] These companies end up saying one thing in their policy statements and another entirely with their political money. Thanks to the lack of transparency and internal controls, their boards and shareholders might not be aware of this reputation-threatening hypocrisy until it shows up in *The New York Times.*

Shareholders understand the risks from corporate political spending, and the majority wholeheartedly support the CPA's proposed reforms. In a survey of American shareholders in March 2006, 85 percent agreed that the "lack of transparency and oversight in corporate political activity" is an incentive for executive mismanagement and threatens the value of their shares. Ninety-four percent were in favor of disclosure; 84 percent supported board oversight and approval of "all direct and indirect [company] political spending."[36] It is a sign of the state of shareholder "democracy" that this overwhelming support translated into 21 percent votes on proxy resolutions.

Despite shareholder pressure, most corporate managers are hostile to the prospect of greater political accountability. They have often suggested that by publicly declaring their guidelines for political contributions, they would be giving the game away to their competitors. The CPA's Richardson has little time for this "competitive disadvantage" excuse. "It's a red herring. . . . Everybody has a pretty good sense of what the emerging regulatory issues are for a given company or industry. And the information we're asking for won't give the company's plans away, because it trails the company's actions. We're not asking for real-time reports, just regular ones."

Most reluctant companies, Richardson adds, simply argue that they don't want to disclose their political spending until all their competitors do. That excuse will grow more threadbare with each year; as in the case of antidiscrimination policy, corporations can resist the tide of mainstream shareholder opinion for only so long. Morgan Stanley was the first company to adopt the CPA's standards for oversight and disclosure, in 2005. Since then, a vanguard of large corporations has begun bowing to investors' demands for political accountability: McDonald's, Staples, Coca-Cola, PepsiCo, drug companies such as Bristol-Myers Squibb and Eli Lilly, Verizon, General Dynamics, American Electric Power, and nine others.[37] These companies, from a wide variety of industries affected by government, have recognized that the benefits of shareholder trust outweigh the minor extra expense or purported competitive disadvantage of disclosure. (All of these transparency pioneers are red, but that's hardly surprising; recall that two thirds of Blue Sector companies don't even have a PAC.)

Richardson sees the political transparency movement developing along the same lines as another major corporate governance issue: expensing stock options. Treating executives' stock options as an expense (like any other form of compensation) was seen as an outlandish minority idea when it was first proposed, but it gained mass shareholder support in the wake of the 2001–2002 corporate scandals and eventually became enshrined in federal accounting standards. "One of our efforts is to continuously create a groundswell of support for this issue," Richardson declares, "and at some point in time it may cause the SEC to sit up and take notice."

We expect accountability and transparency in political contributions to be good for the Blue Sector—not because it's always good business for every company to contribute to Democrats but because so much of the waste, corruption, and unjustifiable spending is currently benefiting the other side. As we showed in Chapter 2, the majority of the money sloshing around in the political system is going to the Republican Party and conservative institutions. Yet red companies as a whole have underperformed the market during the past five years of Republican ascendancy. The verdict is clear: most companies are not creating shareholder value through their political spending. The Republican ideological machine does a lot to obscure this damning fact, but the facts would be clearer to everyone if corporate oversight of political expenditures wasn't so lax and undemanding.

As American progressives work to expand and build up the Blue Sector, we must insist on accountability and transparency as cornerstones of all corporate spending. Blue companies should embrace full political disclosure and be prepared to justify their expenditures to their shareholders and the public at large. We don't want blue company CEOs to follow the example of today's red executives and give shareholders' money to Democrats out of a misguided ideological attachment. Of course, we're preaching to the choir on this one. Blue companies are less than half as likely as red companies to have a PAC in the first place; most of them are blue thanks to their executives' personal contributions. Costco CEO Jim Sinegal says of his own corporation, "We strongly believe you shouldn't be taking shareholders' money and putting it into political causes."[38] While we aren't calling on companies to abolish their PACs, we do believe that business leaders should have an honest, business-related justification for every company dollar they spend on lobbying or political advocacy—and be willing to defend that justification in public.

Giving to Republicans has for too long been its own justification. If shareholders challenge corporate executives more aggressively, asking how their political contributions are linked to a long-term, sustainable business strategy, we expect two welcome trends to emerge: less corporate money going into politics overall and less Republican bias in corporate political contributions.

Lewis Powell understood that shareholders are "the real owners, the real entrepreneurs, the real capitalists under our system." In his seminal 1971 memorandum he lamented their "neglected" power and wondered whether as a group, they could somehow acquire "enough muscle to be influential."[39] Of course, the CEOs who were the real target of Powell's manifesto had no desire to give their shareholders more muscle. Over decades of corporate governance battles, American shareholders have reclaimed some of their neglected power. For the sake of their own investments, it's time they used that power to put the brakes on Powell's financial-political machine.

CHAPTER 8

The Blueprint

Building a Blue Financial Infrastructure

WE'VE DISCUSSED HOW THE REPUBLICAN POLITI-
cal engine is fueled by corporate money, and we've suggested
steps that every progressive can take to drain the Republican
gas tank by expanding the Blue Sector. Just as important as the
fuel, though, is the transmission—the extensive financial infrastructure that transforms money into political power. For the
last thirty-five years, the conservative movement has been
refining its system for channeling money to candidates,
activists, and organizations. We've seen the results over the last
decade; Republicans have repeatedly come out on top in elections, and the framework of American political debate has
shifted several degrees to the right. The conservative movement has had the upper hand not only thanks to its financial support but because it has treated those dollars as *investment*
dollars, the political equivalent of private equity or venture capital, supported by a comprehensive investment infrastructure.

Consider its extraordinary system for incubating new orga-

nizations, ideas, and leaders. Today, a fledgling right-wing political organization can get start-up funding and advice from dozens
of large, professional foundations. It can get grants for research
and advocacy from the U.S. Chamber of Commerce and any
number of politically engaged corporations. Its key staff will benefit from training and paid internships at a variety of Washington
institutes and think tanks. It can mobilize grassroots support
through well-established direct mail and Internet channels—and
can conjure up "AstroTurf" support from organizations that pre-
tend to represent a broad grassroots base but are funded entirely
by grants from corporations and wealthy conservative donors.
Our hypothetical conservative start-up has a ready-made media
platform for making its brand known via conservative radio and
television outlets. Most of its funding will be "general operating
support," not linked to a specific project, allowing it the freedom
to innovate and respond flexibly.

We've only just started to build anything comparable on the
progressive side. Our own political network tends to run on individual passion, short-term program grants, volunteerism, and
single-issue idealism. Even if we succeed in expanding the Blue
Sector and starving the conservative machine of fuel, we badly
need to overhaul our own transmission. Bringing more money
into progressive politics won't help unless we can translate that
money into forward motion: getting our message out to voters,
getting voters to the polls, generating new political ideas and
fresh articulations of old ones, building leadership, mobilizing
activists, and sustaining an extensive ecosystem of progressive
political organizations. To do all that, we'll need a new infrastructure for political investment.

Our old infrastructure was working fine back when Lewis
Powell wrote his memorandum in 1971. Powell was dismayed at

the effectiveness of consumer advocates and environmentalists in setting up new organizations, getting their message out, and influencing legislation on Capitol Hill. He called for corporate America to fund a conservative political infrastructure that would be better organized, better planned, and above all better funded. Today the Republicans have everything Powell envisioned and more; progressives still have more or less the same systems they had in 1971, clearly showing the wear and tear of the last few decades. When the Democrats lost their long-standing control of Congress in 1994, it became painfully clear just how much of their political infrastructure had come to rely on control of Capitol Hill. The progressives' path to leadership had generally begun with a Hill staffing position. Their intellectual and political capital had been focused on single-issue legislative battles, rather than on winning the hearts, minds, and votes of the American electorate—and their money had been similarly divided among dozens of liberal constituencies, rather than mobilized strategically behind a movement.

The contrast to the right was stark. "Having no power in government on an institutional basis, [conservatives] built their own institutional power outside the government," explains Buck Owen, a former vice president at the Democracy Alliance, a league of progressive donors. "For decades, we had the castle and they were storming it. When we lost the castle, there was nowhere to go." As union membership declined and the suburbs and exurbs became more powerful than the old urban political machines, the Democrats' electoral infrastructure could no longer compete with the Republicans'. Our message infrastructure has not kept up with the relentless pace of ideological think tanks like the Heritage Foundation and mass media platforms like FOX News and conservative talk radio. Most important, the financial infrastructure that sustains our broader political network has been fragmented, focused on the short term, cripplingly nonpartisan, and confined by single-issue politics.

That's the bad news. The good news is that progressives have recognized the problem and are applying lessons from the Blue Sector as a blueprint for a new financial infrastructure. Progressive organizations are finally beginning to benefit from the same kind of financial support, management tools, and professional networking that conservatives have long enjoyed. We now have an emerging system of blue venture capital.

Since the conservative machine began churning out election victories, smug Republican critics have often claimed that progressives are simply too disorganized and suspicious of money to build a modern financial-political infrastructure. It's really just another version of the canard that progressives are no good at business. Just as the success of the Blue Sector has blindsided conservative ideologues, we believe that we'll astonish them again with a thriving blue financial infrastructure.

> **Myth: High finance and progressive politics don't mesh.**

Progressives are supposedly allergic to big money. That's an exaggeration, of course, but it's not entirely a myth. Most grassroots progressive constituencies are sensitive to the potential for abuse that comes along with big concentrations of wealth and power. That sensitivity, in fact, is one key reason that progressives tend to be better at running businesses and managing the American economy. Progressive CEOs are more likely to be wary of corner-cutting strategies that will boost the immediate value of their stock options while wrecking the long-term health of the company. Progressive legislators and presidents are less likely to accept naive "trickle-down" theories claiming that whatever is good for Fortune 500 bosses is good for America. Leaders who understand the temptations of corporate power are better able to resist those temptations when it comes to long-term planning and management.

The progressives' skepticism about big money does have its downsides, though. One, which we've already mentioned, is that the well-founded suspicion of corporate power can occasionally slip into the exaggerated belief that all corporations are corrupt and wicked, ignoring the reality of socially responsible business. Another snag is that the progressives' "allergy" to corporate wealth makes it harder to build a solid financial infrastructure for Democratic politics. Many progressive activists are skeptical of the wealthy donors who are interested in funding them; many progressive donors respond defensively to the perceived criticism of their affluence. That sort of mutual wariness may be a recipe for responsible national and corporate governance, but it makes for prickly fund-raising.

Needless to say, the Republicans don't have this problem. The widespread conservative idolatry of the market means that right-wing organizations and activists tend to regard multimillionaires with a kind of reverent awe. In those circles, great wealth is its own justification—indeed, a sign of virtue. All that the chairman of the RNC or other conservative money maestros have to do is bring potential donors into the same room as promising grantees, and the rest will take care of itself. Funding the progressive political network is a much more complicated process, demanding diplomacy and innovation in equal measure.

Small Donors, Rich Donors

Part of the problem, ironically, is that over the last few decades progressives have grown too dependent on big donors. Our ability to raise money from lots of individual small donors was hit particularly hard by the decline in union membership. Meanwhile, the Republicans were the first to take advantage of direct mail as a grassroots fund-raising tool, thanks to Richard Viguerie, one of the most effective political entrepreneurs of the past half century.[1] The archconservative Viguerie helped bankroll the Right by sending out targeted mass mailings with the latest Republican talking points and receiving back tens of thousands of small donor checks.

Since the 2004 election cycle, progressives have begun closing the small-donor gap, disappointing right-wing critics who predicted that "soft money" campaign finance reform would lock out large donors and leave the Democrats bankrupt. The comeback is due largely to a boom in online fund-raising, part of the broader wave of progressive innovation and community-building on the Internet. When it comes to small-donor support, explains Christopher Hayes, editor of the progressive magazine *In These Times,* "the great hope for progressive organizations is that the Internet can be for the left what direct mail has been for the right."[2]

On the Internet the Republicans are the ones playing catchup, while Democrats are the major entrepreneurs. Most Americans have come across MoveOn. Founded by the Silicon Valley entrepreneurs Wes Boyd and Joan Blades, MoveOn is a 3.3-million-member Internet movement that is both a pioneer of online organizing and a powerhouse in the new small-donation political capital markets. Not only did MoveOn raise and spend $25 million (mostly in small donations) to take back the House in

2006, but in the wake of Hurricane Katrina in 2005 it mobilized 16,000 ordinary members to open their homes to fleeing New Orleans residents. "MoveOn is said to have housed more people in the early stages of the disaster than FEMA did."[3]

Less famous but no less innovative are Benjamin Rahn and Matt DeBergalis, who in 2004 launched ActBlue, "the eBay of online fundraising."[4] Just as eBay made Internet auctions straightforward and reliable, drawing millions of ordinary people into e-commerce, ActBlue offers a simple, flexible, and user-friendly platform for progressive fund-raising. The site lists all Democratic candidates for national office (and a fast-growing share of state and local races). Users build their own fund-raising page featuring their favored candidates, with a "contribute" button next to each candidate's blurb, and then invite everyone they know to visit the page and give money.

Like many other great online innovations, ActBlue's architecture is general enough to support a wide variety of passions and priorities. Minnesotans can raise funds for all the key races in Minnesota. Environmental groups can put together a page spotlighting congressional Democrats who support action against climate change. Progressive bloggers can set up a quick-response fund-raising center to bolster Democrats who face an unexpectedly fierce Republican blitz. Democratic candidates themselves can simply link to an ActBlue page rather than having to set up their own Web site to process online contributions. Behind the scenes, ActBlue (a registered PAC) smoothly takes care of all the nuts and bolts: bundling together the contributions from each fund-raising page, dispatching checks to candidates once a week, making sure donors don't exceed their legal campaign finance limits.

Thanks to its early approval by progressive blogs like Daily

Kos, ActBlue has grown by leaps and bounds. Between its launch in June 2004 and the November 2006 elections, ActBlue members raised $17.29 million for Democrats in races across America.[5] ActBlue continues to develop new functions, such as its Presidential Draft Fund, where users begin raising funds for a candidate who *ought* to run for office. (In the event that the candidate doesn't run, the contributions are passed on to the DNC.) The idea of a fund for potential candidates isn't new; what's new is a platform that lets anybody launch such a fund, in a forum where thousands of other small donors can provide an early gauge of popular support.

By empowering every progressive with an Internet connection to be a fundraiser, ActBlue is an emerging leader in the Democrats' small-donor renaissance. Yet we should not treat small donors as a panacea. Conservative organizations have thrived on direct-mail fundraising, but they've benefited far more from a supportive network of ideological foundations fed by enormous corporate and individual contributions. It's easier to mobilize small donors behind specific issues, whether abortion or the environment; big funding institutions are better placed to provide organizations with vital operating support, tied not to single issues but to broader, strategic goals. Big donors are also more likely to take a risk on innovative ideas or organizations. To compete with the right, progressives don't just need to attract more small donors. We need to build institutions that can channel money and expertise from socially responsible businesses (and business executives) to a wide range of the most effective, transformative, or innovative organizations on the left. We need a deep, robust political capital market. Conservative critics can hardly believe it when wealthy progressives contribute extensively to the Democratic cause. It goes against their ideological understanding of the world, in which the interests of the American rich are served exclusively by tax cuts, deregulation, and corporate welfare. The idea that a sustainable, just economy might be better for business—the idea, in other words, that the Blue Sector might really be more profitable than its less responsible red competitors—is beyond the scope of their imagination.

But a cross-class alliance against political and economic irresponsibility should come as no surprise to any student of American history. As the historian Kevin Phillips points out in his meticulous history of American wealth, our country has periodically seen progressive moments in which upper-class reformers such as Theodore Roosevelt, Woodrow Wilson, and Franklin Roosevelt led broad coalitions to limit corporate power in the name of economic and social justice. "When avarice and speculation have run amok, considerable elements of upper-bracket Americans usually joined the political reform camp. Economic class lines simply do not hold, which is part of why wise progressives attack privileges, malefactors, elites, and corruption."[6] Today the stage is set for another such campaign. The progressive passion of many of America's richest financiers and CEOs is genuine; all Americans, whether prosperous, poor, or the dwindling class in between, have a legitimate interest in countering the Republican tide. We must develop the infrastructure that can bring together funds, ideas, and action in a single movement.

The Blue Sector and its leaders will be essential contributors to this new infrastructure—not just as a source of capital but as a source of private-sector insights. The pillars of progressive leadership apply broadly in the political sphere as well. Our blue political network will have the organizational flexibility of the best Blue Sector companies. The new funding institutions we envision will take risks on innovative ideas and organizations. They will take a long-term, strategic view of success and will not contribute money solely for the purpose of winning on specific issues or winning specific elections. A handful of Democratic strategists have already begun building a new financial infrastructure from this blueprint. Over the next decade, we predict that it will drive and sustain a progressive renaissance.

> **Reality: Progressives can back up their ecosystem of political activism with sophisticated finance and the best private-sector management techniques.**

We are witness to a sea change in traditional philanthropy, as billionaires such as Microsoft's Bill Gates and eBay's Pierre Omidyar begin to apply an investment mind-set to their donations. These entrepreneurs have started "allocating their money to make the greatest possible difference to society's problems: in other words, to maximize their 'social return.' Some might operate as relatively hands-off, diversified 'social investors' and some as hands-on, engaged 'venture philanthropists,' the counterparts of mainstream venture capitalists."[7] These donors are determined to produce measurable results, to identify and support innovative "social entepreneurs," and to leverage their donations by linking with the private sector.

Similarly, the first step in overhauling our transmission is for progressives to look at political spending as an investment, not a donation. Kirstin Falk, executive director of the New Progressive Coalition (NPC), an early leader in the new blue financial infrastructure, explains the essential difference in attitude: "Donors have created this transactional relationship, which is basically about getting asked for money, writing a check, and that's it. Investors provide time and expertise, not just money. . . . They have a long time horizon and bring a strategic view of what their money is supposed to accomplish."

We need political venture capitalists who aren't seeking immediate gratification but are looking to support the progressive leaders and organizations that will transform politics in five, ten, or twenty years. We need investors who are willing to take risks on political innovation and won't get discouraged by the failure of any single experiment. We need visionaries who will put their time and money behind good ideas that don't yet have traction and who will champion those ideas all the way into law or policy. Finally, we need to have an understanding of political return on investment—a clear-eyed, nuanced system for judging the impact of the people and groups that we're funding.

The second, related step is to be clear about the nature of the investment. Progressives who invest money in politics need to understand that they are contributing to a *long-term political movement.* That may seem self-evident, but some of the weakest links in our infrastructure stem from the surprising failure to appreciate that three-word description of what political investment is about. It's not just about winning the next election. It is about partisan politics. It is about a movement, not just a collection of specific issues.

Short-Term, Nonpolitical, Single-Issue Donors

Progressives need a reservoir of money. Right now, we have a monsoon. Every couple years, our flow of political money builds to a flood in the fall, then dries up after the first Tuesday in November. Much of the money that feeds our progressive infrastructure is tied to specific, short-term projects, and when the project is finished, the grantee organizations are left scrambling for new donors.

The Republicans, by contrast, are sitting on an aquifer that is repeatedly topped up by conservative megadonors and corporations. Their spending also peaks at election time, of course, but they have access to millions of dollars year in and year out, all earmarked for conservative causes. They understand that politics isn't just about winning this election year but sustaining the institutions that will help them win the next four elections. As a result, less of their funding is tied to short-term projects, and more of it is in long-term operating support. The National Committee for Responsive Philanthropy's report on the conservative Axis of Ideology documents their success:

> Conservative foundations are more likely to create new organizations and fund them for the long-haul, sometimes for decades, not just years, allowing the organizations to focus on their program work, rather than having to worry about where next year's (or month's) budget will come from.[8]

That ties into the next problem: too many progressive organizations are obliged to rely on nonpolitical funding. This is especially true of nonprofit groups that are a step or two removed from outright political activism—organizations that try to document unethical labor conditions, say, or provide voter services to Hispanic immigrants. Too many of these groups receive their funding from large nonpartisan institutions like the Ford Foundation or Rockefeller Foundation, which, despite their general progressive outlook, "live in fear of being hauled before Congress, nailed by the IRS, or mau-maued by right-wing critics for any perceived political project."[9] These foundations have a strong preference for project funding, and they are unlikely to approve projects with an overt political slant.

By contrast, the big conservative foundations like Koch, Smith Richardson, and Coors are explicitly and passionately political. Without fear of backlash, the right-wing billionaire Richard Mellon Scaife has poured his family money into "general operating" grants for the Heritage Foundation, the Federalist Society, Judicial Watch, and innumerable other actively political conservative groups—not to mention the millions of dollars he spent digging for negative information on Bill Clinton during the 1990s.[10]

We can't base a movement on the support of nonpartisan institutions. For one thing, they're running scared. The conservative movement relentlessly attacks mainstream American institutions for being biased against their ideas—not only big donors like Ford, but television broadcasters like CBS, newspapers like *The Washington Post,* and think tanks like the Brookings Institution. These institutions have historically seen themselves as nonpartisan; Brookings in particular was founded on the principle that "day to day government was not a matter of political emotionalism, but of quiet competence and professionalism,"[11] a description that rang painfully false in the Washington of Bush and DeLay. Unsurprisingly, such organizations have shrunk away from the right-wing assault. In their place, in the name of "balance," the conservatives have erected expressly ideological institutions: FOX News, the American Enterprise Institute, the Bradley Foundation, and so on down the list.

We don't want reputable nonpartisan organizations and foundations to acquire an actual progressive bias. Heaven knows it's a good thing to have media and intellectual institutions that try to identify truth without imposing a preset partisan agenda. There are plenty of worthy nonpolitical causes that deserve foundation funding. But if the major institutional participants in the American political process are all either self-identified nonpartisans or zealous conservatives, the discussion is going to move in a predictable direction. The progressive movement must create an explicitly political infrastructure that can stand up to the right-wing onslaught. We especially need large funding bodies that won't shrink from accusations of partisanship. As Lewis Powell emphasized back in 1971, if you're going to mobilize money behind your political values, you need funders who aren't afraid to think politically.

Finally, progressive investors need to understand that they're financing a movement, which takes priority over any single issue or constituency. During the Democrats' decades-long stint as the majority party in Congress, the progressive infrastructure became increasingly balkanized. Because we didn't have to unite in a serious struggle for control of Congress, each progressive constituency could focus the lion's share of its efforts on its favored issue. Our financial infrastructure evolved into clusters of donors supporting a specific concern. Many of the most powerful 527s on the left—EMILY's List, the League of Conservation Voters—are single-issue or single-constituency groups. Even progressive organizations with a more general mandate end up receiving much of their money with issue-specific strings attached.

The tangle from these strings can be particularly damaging during election season. When the Democrats need to run ads in

Ohio, for example, they would naturally like to highlight a locally crucial issue such as job losses. Too often, however, progressive organizations are bound by the conditions of their funding to a specific agenda or demographic—advertising to Hispanic voters, for example, or on environmental causes. While these are important issues, they are unlikely to determine the votes of swing voters. We have hobbled ourselves by tying our money and our activism too closely to issues and not to victory. In a world where the Democrats have to fight hard for a majority in either house of Congress, this is self-defeating even for single-issue constituencies. As the progressive bloggers Jerome Armstrong and Markos Moulitsas Zúniga insist in their recent manifesto for Democrats, "no one's narrow agenda is served by being in the minority . . . a governing majority would mean far more for everyone's pet causes than a hostile, entrenched, dominant Republican majority." [12]

By contrast, big conservative donors generally give money without earmarks; they want their 501(c) and 527 groups to put out whatever message will win the race. The various Republican constituencies—CEOs in New York, religious conservatives in Alabama, libertarian ranchers in Wyoming, tax-cut fanatics in Washington D.C.—have long been able to paper over their differences in the name of larger strategic goals such as taking and holding Congress. The biggest evangelical power brokers (such as James Dobson and Ralph Reed) have been willing to sacrifice their favored social issues temporarily in the name of electoral victory for the overall conservative movement. Right-wing financiers such as Scaife and the Olin and Bradley Foundations have strategically spread their funding across a broad, contradictory swathe of the conservative spectrum, from the libertarian Cato Institute to the influential theocon journal *First Things*. [13]

This focus and strategic unity can be harder to maintain when you are the party in power. Even some right-wing Republicans can engage in self-destructive feuding. Grover Norquist's Club for Growth, whose overriding issue is tax cuts, targeted moderate Republican candidates across the country in 2006; its primary broadside against the insufficiently ideological Rhode Island Senator Lincoln Chafee was one of the many factors that cost the GOP control of the Senate in 2006.[14] Closed-border, anti-immigrant campaigners like Colorado's Tom Tancredo ferociously attacked fellow Republicans who argued for some version of an economically sensible guest worker program. As a result, in fall 2006 "after years of trending Republican the national Latino vote swung very heavily towards the Democrats."[15] Religious Right leaders grumble that their puritanical vision for America is as far from fulfillment as ever, even under an evangelical president and until recently a like-minded Congress. The humiliating rebuke of the 2006 elections has tied up the conservative movement in a snarl of mutual recrimination.

But we progressives would be foolish to expect this disarray to last for long. Having lost the castle, the Republicans can still rally around the independent institutions they built up during their long siege and come back harder than ever. We need to shore up our own unity if we're going to withstand the next conservative surge. We cannot forget the lessons of the early 2000s, when Democrats found themselves a minority in every branch of government. None of our many internal disagreements is as challenging as the gulf between libertarians and evangelicals within the Republican Party. We can unite as a movement behind basic progressive ideals: equality of opportunity, a constructive role for government, protection against discrimination, and an economic policy that is prudent, sustainable, and just. We must take a strategic political view that goes beyond our individual constituencies and aims for the victory of a broadly progressive coalition under the Democratic big tent.

Thankfully, the progressive years in the wilderness and the innumerable offenses of the George W. Bush administration have concentrated a lot of minds on the left. After the 2004 defeat of John Kerry, a wide range of Democrats realized that we urgently needed an infrastructure overhaul and that in particular we needed a better system for mobilizing money behind our movement. Since then, we have seen the first conscious attempts to build progressive parallels to the conservative financial institutions inspired by the Powell Memorandum.

A Democratic Aquifer

The apostle of the new wave of blue capital is Rob Stein, a long-time Democratic strategist and adviser to former DNC Chairman Ron Brown. Stein was not the first to grasp that a potent financial infrastructure was key to the success of the conservative political machine. But he dug up the details, from Lewis Powell to the right-wing blogosphere, and condensed them into a now semilegendary PowerPoint presentation, "The Conservative Message Machine Money Matrix." With strong support from Simon Rosenberg, founder of the New Politics Institute, and the NDN, Stein took his message on the road in 2003 and 2004.

By the time George W. Bush came out on top in Ohio in the 2004 presidential election, Stein had convinced many of the most generous progressive investors to create an aquifer of capital to match the strategic, long-term political funding available to the Right. The disheartening election results were the catalyst that turned their vision into an institution. In early 2005, Stein helped organize several dozen wealthy, determined progressives into a new funding coalition to reshape the political infrastructure of the left: the Democracy Alliance.

The Alliance is essentially a forum for more than a hundred of the largest contributors on the Left to coordinate their giving and provide strategic support to key progressive organizations. It aims at mobilizing the very top tier of wealthy political investors; every partner reportedly agrees to pay an initial $25,000 fee, $30,000 in annual dues, and a minimum of $200,000 per year to the Alliance's select organizations.[16] The partners meet twice a year to deliberate over which groups should be eligible for Alliance funding. They eventually generate a consensus list of recommended organizations, and individual partners decide how to divide their $200,000 among the potential beneficiaries.

In choosing which groups are recommended, the Alliance has taken up Stein's appeal for a focus on infrastructure to reinforce progressives and strengthen areas where we are currently weaker than conservatives. The Alliance aims to provide groups with general operating support, not limited program grants. In theory, the funding is also long term—though because individual partners make the ultimate check-writing decisions each year, the Alliance's long-term pledges are in practice only as solid as the partners' continued commitment to their chosen groups. Like the big right-wing foundations, the Alliance invests in groups across the progressive spectrum. Many of its partners have a particular interest in organizations that go "beyond the Beltway" and operate on a national or multistate scale.

The Democracy Alliance is a vital experiment, taking blue finance into unknown, sometimes rocky territory. The organization has faced the start-up challenges that one might expect when you put dozens of strong-willed millionaires and billionaires together in a room and try to bring them to a consensus. It also famously chose to operate with a high degree of opacity even for the foundation world. The Alliance did not initially encourage applicants; indeed, it deliberately chose not to have a Web site, did not issue press releases, and generally discouraged both partners and beneficiaries from broadcasting their Alliance affiliation. According to Buck Owen, the organization's former vice president, this caution was primarily due to the desire not to be overwhelmed by applications for Alliance recognition. Many partners also hoped to avoid the intense partisan fire drawn by George Soros and other wealthy individual donors during the 2004 election cycle.

Unfortunately the Democracy Alliance discovered that lack of transparency can strain relations with one's own allies. The Alliance's initial opacity about its criteria for consideration and approval alienated many progressive organizations; these potential beneficiaries were alarmed that tremendous streams of funding were being channeled based on discussions they could neither affect nor appeal. By its second round of funding in May 2006, the Alliance had set up an application process that drew in a much wider range of progressive groups.[17]

The results so far have been promising. Some of the Alliance's recommended organizations (the Sierra Club, the Center for American Progress) are well-established institutions, key nodes in the progressive network. Others are little-known but promising groups that suddenly find their good work thrust into the spotlight.

Creating a leadership pipeline, for example, as one of these groups does, is exactly the sort of farsighted infrastructure work that won't make headlines but will eventually make an important difference. "Having this college kid go attend the two-day training to learn how to be an inner-city political organizer, how to navigate the political machinations within Pennsylvania—it's not something Congress is going to be debating," says Owen. "This is much more subtle, long term. It's an investment in people, not an investment in running television ads. And it will continue to pay dividends, probably mostly unnoticed," through leaders working at the local level or behind the scenes on major campaigns.

As the first fruit of Rob Stein's broader consciousness-raising campaign, the Democracy Alliance has finally got progressives working seriously on long-term infrastructure investment—critical as we strive to create political markets where the best ideas win out. The Alliance is an invaluable forum for big political investors to discuss strategy, share information, and mobilize money behind the movement. And because of its novelty, its opacity, and its multimillion-dollar scale, the Alliance has drawn lots of press attention over the past two years. Whether it thrives or falters, however, the Alliance is only the first word in the progressive response to the right's financial infrastructure. "It's not the equivalent of the whole conservative machine," Owen says. "It needs to be one piece of a much bigger puzzle."

Blue Venture Capital

The New Progressive Coalition (NPC) is another major new institution inspired by Stein's analysis of the conservative money matrix. If the Democracy Alliance can be called the private-equity giant of progressive political investment—making massive investments in select institutions, based on an appraisal of their long-term strategic value—then NPC can be called the venture capital outfit, mobilizing smaller investments behind a multitude of promising new ideas. Its founders, the Bay Area business leaders Andrew and Deborah Rappaport, want to infuse the progressive financial infrastructure with the ethos of Silicon Valley venture capitalism: putting money behind hundreds of new groups, expecting many of them to fail or flag but knowing that some of them will catch fire and justify all the money spent.[18]

NPC has accordingly thrown open its doors to hundreds of progressive member organizations, some of them experienced, most of them less than five years old. The NPC Web site is a one-stop shop where organizations can get advice and useful resources, find out what other like-minded groups are up to, and make their pitch to potential investors. For example, the Web site offers "Guides to Not Re-Inventing the Wheel" for new organizations, providing an institutional memory for the progressive network. Members can get answers to their questions from "How do we do our grassroots training with limited resources?" to "What's an independent audit, and when do we need one?" Organizations can also sign up for teleseminars and conferences, drawing on NPC's advisory team of more than sixty specialists. The NPC team offers comprehensive advice and support to start-up members, helping them find capital, overcome legal and organizational hurdles, access the best technical and managerial tools available, and build coalitions to leverage their efforts.

For progressive investors, on the other hand, NPC acts as a blue investment advisory service, providing a road map through the maze of potential grantees. It breaks down the universe of possible progressive recipients into six sectors—advocacy, electoral work, idea generation, infrastructure building, leadership, and media—and publishes regular sector briefs to help investor members keep abreast of what's going on in each area. A few of NPC's investor members (including the Rappaports) are generous and wealthy on a Democracy Alliance scale, megadonors who can commit millions of dollars to promising if risky new organizations. But for the most part NPC doesn't aim that high, nor for the small donor base at the other end of the scale. Rather, according to NPC Executive Director Kirstin Falk, the coalition focuses on mobilizing the next generation of political investors—young professionals who can contribute a few thousand dollars now but will be able to invest much more as they advance in their careers. If NPC can inspire its more than two hundred investor members with the Rappaports' passion for innovation, it will give a huge boost to the next generation of progressive capital markets.

NPC recognized early on, however, that investors were reluctant to embrace the venture capital mind-set without a better way of measuring return on investment. Investors were afraid to pick risky investments and wanted to be able to track the performance of the groups they supported—but they weren't sure how to sort out the useful metrics from the flood of available information. "What we heard from both sides of the equation is that investors have no way to monitor their investments," Falk explained. "So they usually just act based on what their friends tell them. Often that sends them to large, established organizations that in some cases may not even be part of the solution anymore."

Meanwhile, NPC's member organizations were also suffering from the lack of clear success metrics. Many found themselves having to focus on fashionable areas outside their core competence to attract funding. If in a particular year investors were fixated on keeping progressives from "losing the media battle," organizations had to put money into a media program, whether or not it was actually relevant to their work. In an election year, organizations felt pressure to show that their work was relevant to the election results—even groups like think tanks and leadership training institutes, whose objectives must be measured on a much longer time scale. Most organizations were eager to develop a way of identifying and measuring achievements that was consistent and specific to their sector.

To meet this need, NPC brought together representatives from all sides—political investors, investment experts, a wide range of progressive organizations—and tasked them with developing a system for measuring "political return on investment." A few core measures of success, such as cost-effectiveness and program replicability, were the same for all groups; others varied by sector. Idea generation organizations would be judged on measures like the impact of their ideas on legislation and their publication rate. Leadership development groups would be judged partly on how many people pass through their programs and partly on how successful those graduates are at getting into top jobs.

When the project is up and running, progressive political investors will be able, for the first time, to rate the performance of their investments through objective, sector-appropriate comparisons. NPC will also be able to roll out "political mutual funds," portfolios of progressive political organizations whose success is tracked using the political return on investment metrics. Like stock market mutual funds, these portfolios will exist to spread and manage risk; political investors will be able to put their money into a wide range of organizations with the confidence that the money won't be wasted if one or two groups go belly-up.

This is the sort of crucial innovation that will bring progressive capital markets up to par with the long-standing Republican money machine, both in quality and quantity. Between the small-donor renaissance represented by MoveOn and ActBlue, the big money mustered by the Democracy Alliance and individual blue-company billionaires, and the venture capitalist mentality of NPC, the financial infrastructure of the progressive movement is already in dramatically better health than it was only five years ago. Progressive political financiers are adopting the long-term investment mentality and passion for innovation that has made Blue Sector CEOs so successful.

When we turn to the next generation of progressive organizations, we see that there, too, the pillars of progressive leadership play an essential role. In particular, the benefits of a flat, decentralized organizational structure will be key for the future course of our movement.

CHAPTER 9

The Progressive Ecosystem

SO FAR, WE'VE USED PLENTY OF MECHANICAL META-
phors to describe our progressive infrastructure: gas tanks,
transmissions, engines of political activism. A successful political movement is more than just an election-winning, law-passing
machine, though. In many ways, we'd do better to think of it as
an ecosystem. Whereas an ecosystem consists of diverse
species, a political movement has diverse sectors: idea generation, grassroots mobilization, getting a message out in the
media, law and policy advocacy, leadership training, and so on.
Organizations in each sector feed off the work of the other sectors. When one sector grows weak or falls behind, all the others
feel the impact. Every once in a while, one sector evolves into
something startlingly new, creating echoes throughout the rest
of the political ecosystem.

We prefer this ecological metaphor to the industrial-age
mechanistic ones because it dispels illusions of control. When
we talk about our political infrastructure as a machine, we are

implying that we can consciously design it, upgrade its parts, and make it do more or less what we want. That's an adequate enough way to describe some of our institutions and some of our sectors. But when we get to the level of the movement as a whole, to the full sweep of progressive organizations, the mechanistic metaphors fall apart. The movement wasn't designed, and it can't be controlled. New ideas, new challenges, whole new sectors are constantly evolving. If we try to restrain it, we may find it easier to manage, but we might also stifle the innovation that could move the whole system forward to a new level.

Our choice of metaphors affects how we think about the progressive movement's reputed disorganization. Many readers will have heard of Will Rogers's quip "I'm not a member of any organized political party—I'm a Democrat." These days more than ever, there's a widespread sense that progressives just can't get organized, that we're a clutter of fragmented, single-interest constituencies masquerading as a political movement. The Republicans, by contrast, are seen as systematic and disciplined, rather like an army or a well-oiled machine. There's some truth in both those caricatures, which we've already explored in earlier chapters, but they cover a deeper falsehood. In reality, the conservative and progressive movements are moving toward different styles of organization, and over the long haul, the progressive style will prove stronger.

> **Myth: The Democrats can't organize as effectively as the Republicans.**

The success of the Blue Sector shows that there's nothing inherently disordered or ineffective about a progressive ethos.

Business leaders who favor the Democrats are no less organized than their red counterparts. As we saw back in Chapter 4, though, there's a difference in the *style* of organization favored by blue companies. Progressive firms are more willing to experiment with a decentralized, flexible organizational structure that encourages creativity and boosts participation by employees and customers alike. They're also more likely to adopt novel forms of organization, like Whole Foods' self-regulating team structure or Progressive Insurance's periodic shuffling of positions.

We think the same pattern holds true for progressive political organizations and for our political infrastructure as a whole. The progressive movement is by nature decentralized, a network rather than a machine. That can be infuriating when bits of it aren't working together as smoothly as we might want, and it puts the movement beyond the control of any one leader or group. But that diverse openness also makes our movement as a whole more adaptable, inventive, and viable over the long term. In politics, or any other sphere where creativity and innovation are decisive skills, a hierarchical organizational structure can pretty reliably get you "B"-grade results. Decentralization can collapse into disorganization (a "D" grade), but with the right caliber of leadership, it also creates the possibility of getting and maintaining an "A."

The Democratic Party used to be a more hierarchical, vertically integrated organization back when labor unions were stronger and urban party machines were at their height. In those days the unions and the party power brokers administered the progressive movement from the center. Today, even if we progressives succeed in helping to revive unions from their long slump, the progressive movement won't go back to its old organizational style. The most successful unions of today are themselves more flexible and less centralized, and in today's diverse progressive movement, the Democratic Party cannot provide executive leadership. Rather, the progressive movement can learn from the Blue Sector how to devolve power to the ground level and break up old infrastructure.

Back in Chapter 4, for instance, we saw how the blue innovator Forest Laboratories rejected the vertically integrated norm of the pharmaceutical industry. Instead of trying to do everything itself, from R&D to licensing to marketing, Forest cut back on its own original drug research. Instead of seeing other pharmaceutical companies solely as competitors, it identified some as partners and put its energy into licensing and promoting its drugs in the U.S. market. This division of labor gave Forest a striking competitive advantage over its rivals, which still tried to keep everything in-house. In the same way, the Democratic Party and the new progressive mass organizations (like MoveOn) and donor coalitions (like the Democracy Alliance) should see each other not as rivals but as partners, building a movement on the strengths of each. A decentralized coalition is more likely to sustain the wave of progressive political participation and innovation that has characterized the last five years.

Amway Versus the Gate-crashers

The Republican political capital markets have generated plenty of innovation over the last few decades, but the conservatives' most distinctive advances (such as direct mail as a fund-raising tool and talk radio as a media outlet) have served a fundamentally hierarchical machine, where control remains as centralized as possible. For example, in the 2004 election the GOP transformed its get-out-the-vote operation, taking a loose volunteer structure and turning it into a tightly organized pyramid. Each layer of volunteers was responsible for recruiting and managing the layer below it. Each volunteer had hard, specific targets for how many volunteers to recruit and how many voters to contact, in a plan sent down and monitored from Bush campaign headquarters in Arlington, Virginia. The result, RNC Chair Ken Mehlman agreed, was a multilevel marketing scheme like Amway's, except instead of dietary supplements, this organization was selling the Bush administration.[1]

New York Times reporter Matt Bai spent time inside the Republicans' novel Ohio campaign and was struck by the level of centralized control in what was theoretically a grassroots system. "The more time I spent with these volunteer leaders, the more apparent it became that . . . they were not, in fact, empowered to make even minuscule adjustments to the Plan. In fact, the campaign was conducted entirely by conference calls—among regional chairmen, county chairmen, coalition chairmen—that enabled aides at headquarters in Virginia to direct virtually every facet of the Ohio strategy."[2] The new structure was unquestionably innovative and even successful, but at the end of the day, it took away power from most of its participants.

By contrast, the latest wave of Democratic political innovation has by and large created a more decentralized party with an egalitarian, participatory culture. In the same way that blue companies have been more willing to work constructively with advocacy groups, the progressive movement has shown itself more willing to adapt to disruptive new ideas from the grass roots. Most Democratic leaders embraced the Internet's potential for increased popular participation as soon as they understood its implications. The Democrats' instincts are genuinely to be the party of the people, even when a new opportunity disrupts the status quo. The results over the past few years have been clear: progressives, rather than conservatives, have generated and adopted the innovations that have expanded political participation for ordinary voters.

For instance, take the new surge in progressive small-donor fund-raising enabled by online institutions like ActBlue and MoveOn. The distinctive thing about these groups isn't that they use the Internet to raise money; anyone can do that, and plenty of conservatives do. Their innovation was giving individual donors and members leeway to determine the direction in which their money goes. Anybody can set up an ActBlue contribution page or presidential draft fund for the candidates of his or her choice. Any MoveOn member can participate in the online forums that set the organization's priorities and strategies.

On the media side, to take another example, both parties are well represented in the blogosphere. There's a crucial difference, however, between the biggest progressive blog (Daily Kos) and the biggest right-wing ones (InstaPundit, Michelle Malkin), and it isn't only that Daily Kos reaches more than four times as many people in an average week.[3] The star conservative bloggers generally offer a lecture—an abbreviated, hyperlinked version of familiar tirades from right-wing talk show hosts or FOX News commentators. Most of them don't allow comments on their posts. Progressive blogs like Daily Kos, by contrast, not only encourage comment and criticism but help readers join, start their own "diaries" linked to the main blog, and engage in independent conversation, activism, and political organizing. These blogs link not only to other "message" sites but also to a broader network of offline advocacy and action. In short, the major progressive blogs are actual communities and offer more opportunities for participation.[4] That's why, as we saw in Chapter 6, they can be so useful in mobilizing people for "real-world" consumer and political activism.

As Simon Rosenberg, founder of NDN, has said for years, the progressive movement's decentralized, participatory organizational structure is really a long-term advantage. When we asked Kirstin Falk, executive director of the New Progressive Coalition, whether the new generation of blue infrastructure would basically look and operate just like the Republican political machine, she immediately and emphatically said no. "It's very important to acknowledge what has worked for the conservatives," Falk allows. "But the progressive machine has different dynamics—how we operate versus how they operate. They are very top down, and that's been very successful for them. But in today's world, it's increasingly hard to run a top-down machine. We're more comfortable in a distributed approach than they are . . . and ultimately, our network approach will outperform their hierarchy."

Reality: Democrats are ahead of Republicans in creating a next-generation network of decentralized, participatory, and innovative political organizations.

We don't want to inadvertently echo Oscar Wilde. Wilde's plays are full of vain characters who paint their weaknesses and vices as strengths; as Algernon in *The Importance of Being Earnest* says of his piano skills, "I don't play accurately—anyone can play accurately—but I play with wonderful expression." We've basically just said that "progressives don't organize in a centralized, hierarchical way—even Republicans can do that—but we organize with wonderful participation." Some critics might suspect that we're just trying to put a pretty face on the progressive movement's disorder. What's the difference between being decentralized and being disorganized?

There are two essential factors that turn an ineffective shambles into a creative, dynamic network: the right kind of leadership, and the right kind of interconnections. We wouldn't argue with anyone who says that our progressive political infrastructure needs *more* of both factors. But we're heading in the right direction—unlike the Republicans, who under Karl Rove, George W. Bush, and Tom DeLay worked hard to centralize power and marginalize any messages they didn't like (including from their own allies, advisers, and grass roots).

"Legislative" Leadership and Constructive Coalitions

Take leadership, the first factor. It's just as important in a "flat" organization as in a traditional, top-down machine. In a decentralized network, though, an effective leader does not *control* so much as *catalyze*.[5] A good leader inspires new connections among independent, self-organizing groups and brings out each group's distinctive strength. She or he will set a direction for the movement that people will follow because they believe in it, not because they are compelled to. A large-enough network will generate multiple leaders, who reinforce one another and find new opportunities for mutual growth. Needless to say, this takes the kind of leadership that puts ego second to a greater purpose.

The management guru Jim Collins, in his famous book *Good to Great*, praised ego-free leadership as one key factor in a company's leap to greatness.[6] Less famously, Collins also wrote

a small book aimed at leaders of "social sector" organizations—
churches, charities, advocacy organizations, government agencies—which are generally much less centralized than
corporations. In it, Collins specifically addresses the difference
between leaders who control and leaders who catalyze:

> [T]here are are two types of leadership skill: *executive*
> and *legislative*. In executive leadership, the individual
> leader has enough concentrated power to simply make
> the right decisions. In legislative leadership, on the
> other hand, no individual leader—not even the nominal
> chief executive—has enough structural power to make
> the most important decisions by himself or herself. Leg-
> islative leadership relies more upon persuasion, political
> currency, and shared interests to create the conditions
> for the right decisions to happen.[7]

The Bush administration and the recently ousted Republican
Congress understood only one model of leadership: complete
concentration of decision-making power in their hands. They
showed no skill or interest in a "legislative," catalyzing, consul-
tative leadership style. We know that our first MBA president
was trying to style his government after a corporate boardroom.
Yet Jim Collins warns business leaders not to mistake "executive" leadership for the best corporate management style. He
predicts that in business as in other spheres, "the most effective
leaders will show a blend of *both* executive and legislative
skills," especially as the raw power of CEOs diminishes in the
face of today's legal, social, and economic changes.[8]

Progressives, on the other hand, have a natural affinity for
collaborative, catalytic leadership. We've seen how progressive

CEOs have embraced an organization structure that involves widespread participation and devolved decision making. Think of Whole Foods putting the company's health plan to a vote of all 25,000 employees or of Google's founders seeking input from employees in their weekly companywide Q&A session. Similarly, the progressive political movement has developed stellar leaders who form strong coalitions and who bring out the best in other groups. Think of Howard Dean, current chair of the DNC, who has worked hard to devolve power to the state-level Democratic Party organizations and build bridges to the many constituents of the progressive movement. Dean is tough and ambitious, and he certainly doesn't lack executive skills, but he also has an intuitive sense for team building and inspiring people to share his vision.

The second factor that makes decentralization work is abundant, constructive *interconnection* between the groups in the network. The groups need more than just a vague sense of common identity. They need information about what other groups are doing to build on each other's work. They must have enough trust to form coalitions and long-term collaborative relationships. The more the groups operate at arm's length from one another, the less effective the network will be.

In the words of the New Progressive Coalition, the movement needs to be "wired." The Rappaports applied two key metaphors from their Silicon Valley background when they founded NPC. The first, which we discussed in the last chapter, was political donations as venture capitalism. The second was the progressive movement as a poorly managed network, with hundreds of flourishing nodes of activism, talent, and resources but weak or nonexistent links connecting the nodes. The Rappaports saw too many organizations duplicating other organizations' work and too few collaborating constructively. New groups lacked the capital and expertise to get off the ground, while political investors lacked reliable, big-picture information about the progressive infrastructure to guide their funding decisions. All these nodes needed to be wired up in a way that would create a marketplace of ideas and action. "We don't want to compete with existing hubs," NPC Executive Director Falk emphasizes. "We want to link them, to turn a network into a movement."

The challenge is to prove that we can form functional coalitions without top-down control by a Washington strategist like Karl Rove. We need to show that our distributed network really can generate enough innovation to outperform the Republican machine. To do that, we'll need deep and constructive collaboration, not just a bunch of brilliant individual groups. "A single well-run organization cannot revitalize the sense that our party is going somewhere," warns Rachel Kleinfeld, executive director of the Truman National Security Project, an innovative national security strategy center. "A group of groups that have got it together well enough to really work together, strategize together, execute together and apart, can get people excited. It can make Democrats feel that their party is capable of functioning."

We suggest that on these issues, the Blue Sector has essential lessons for our political movement. Our political infrastructure is currently weak on two of the pillars of progressive leadership: Pillar IV (investment in employees' well-being) and Pillar V (constructive relationships with critics). These pillars are crucial because they link back directly to the two factors that strengthen us as a decentralized movement: leadership and interconnection. If we don't invest in the young people currently working in progressive organizations, our movement will wind up with a weaker generation of leaders. If our political organizations can't form constructive relationships with progressive critics, our movement won't develop connections at the deep level, where they matter most. Without those pillars, progressives can build any number of innovative, successful groups, but those groups won't add up to a movement.

Applying the Pillars to Politics

To strengthen Pillar IV, progressive groups must invest in employees through proper compensation, mentoring, and training. The staff of progressive organizations today are the executive directors, top political strategists, and electoral candidates of tomorrow. The Democrats have plenty of infrastructure set up to support those leaders once they get to the candidate stage, but we don't offer them much of a career path before that point. By contrast, the conservative political machine is, among many other things, a professional development ladder, with plenty of funding to subsidize young leaders as they build their résumés. As Armstrong and Moulitsas put it in *Crashing the Gate:* "Republicans are taking care of their young stars, funneling them into places where they can have the most impact, be it academic, the punditry, media, or elected office, while we starve our young."[9]

Investors in progressive organizations often come from the private sector themselves and ought to understand the need for competitive salaries and professional development. Volunteerism is an important part of the progressive movement, but it can't be the backbone of our political infrastructure. Progressives understand this just fine when it comes to public school teachers. We've historically supported public education in the face of constant right-wing attempts to slash its funding. We don't assume that intelligent young professionals will become high school teachers just because they love the job; we know that we need to pay them a reasonable salary and give them job security. Why do we think that intelligent young professionals will run our political infrastructure for less?

On the bright side, when we do produce leaders, we tend to produce ones who are well suited to decentralized, catalytic leadership. As we have said, progressive leaders tend to favor a far more collaborative approach and their instincts are team-oriented and egalitarian. And, thankfully, a growing number of progressive investors and organizations are now recognizing the need to foster future leaders. In the last chapter we mentioned the fine work of the Center for Progressive Leadership, supported in part through the Democracy Alliance. NPC is also publicizing the problem and working to remedy it. One core metric in its political return on investment project is, How much of the budget is dedicated to professional development? NPC has also hosted an executive director series to help young organizational leaders meet and discuss solutions to the challenges of progressive leadership.

The second weak pillar—the ability to build constructive relationships with progressive critics—is just as valuable to blue political organizations as it is to the Blue Sector. It's true that few progressive political groups are accused by other progressive groups of destroying the environment or exploiting workers overseas. But the relationships between groups are still often critical, even antagonistic. There are many competing visions for the progressive movement, and our political ecosystem has to be robust enough to deal with some profound disagreements.

In the business world, as we saw in Chapter 5, Blue Sector CEOs are more likely to overcome the natural human response to criticism—defensiveness and hostility—and recognize advocacy groups as potential partners in developing a better progressive business model. In the same way, the leaders of progressive political organizations need to form coalitions with critics and rivals, seeing other groups not primarily as threats to their vision or competitors for resources but as partners in shaping a broader movement.

We've mentioned already that the conservative movement did a good job at this during its long years in the political wilderness. The Christian Coalition and the libertarian, tax cut side of the movement threw a few brickbats at each other, but for the most part they were able to collaborate fruitfully despite their major areas of disagreement. By contrast, during the decades when progressive groups could take a Democratic Congress for granted, the relations between them became more competitive and argumentative. The groups were rivals for a smaller pool of progressive financial support—thanks in part to the red shift in corporate America that sent most of its money to the right-wing political infrastructure.

Fortunately, we sense a coming sea change. Right now there's a real perception of scarcity and competition within the progressive political infrastructure, Falk admits. But we are convinced, having spent time with so many progressive leaders, that the next generation of progressives who are running institutions and making investments think differently—they see that there's no choice but to collaborate. We are also hopeful that the new blue financial infrastructure has already begun to reduce the sense of scarcity and funding insecurity in the progressive movement.

So much for the two weaker pillars—what about the other four? Ecoefficiency is less of a distinguishing factor among progressive political groups, where most of the participants are environmentally responsible and few have an ecofootprint on par with that of a big company. On the remaining three pillars, however, the up-and-coming generation of progressive infrastructure holds many outstanding and inspiring performers. These groups (most of which are five years old or younger) tend to be innovative and organizationally decentralized and are working toward a long-term vision. They show how the pillars of progressive leadership will be a firm underpinning for the future success of the progressive movement.

Pillar I: A Culture of Innovation

We've already seen that the rising generation of blue political infrastructure is nothing if not innovative. As with Blue Sector companies, some of the best-known examples are Internet innovators like MoveOn, ActBlue, and Daily Kos, but the general trend of blue creativity goes far deeper. Consider the perennial problem of voter mobilization; when we manage to get more youth, minorities, and working-class voters to the polls, Democrats win, but when Republican voter suppression efforts succeed, we lose. Many of the innovative contributions from young progressive groups have gone into getting more people registered and making sure their votes count.

For example, Mobile Voter is using cell phone technology "to make registering to vote as easy as calling a friend." [10] Roughly three quarters of Americans now own a cell phone, but few political organizations from either side of the spectrum have figured out how to put this nearly ubiquitous technology to use. [11] That isn't true abroad. In Spain, the 2004 general election was swayed at the last minute by mass demonstrations, organized on the fly by cell phone text messages. On election day, cell phone text messages in Spain surged by 40 percent, summoning absentee voters to the polls and contributing to a surprise victory by the left-wing opposition.[12] Mobile Voter was founded that year and has since been pioneering political text messaging in America.

We thought we'd try out its voter registration systems by texting "voter" to 75444. Within seconds, we received the following message:

> Thx! Now txt back ur email
> addr 2 get ur voter reg form.
> TxtVoter.org is a nonpartisan
> nonprofit 4 voter reg. Ur std
> txt rates aply

When we texted back our e-mail address, we received another message:

> Congrats! You'll get ur
> voter reg form email soon.
> We'll txt u on Election Day
> 2 remind u 2 vote. opt-out
> by replying 'end'.
> Otherwise, enjoy!

It's a simple idea, but in 2006 it won Mobile Voter a Wireless Innovation Award and a major George Washington University grant to boost youth voter turnout. In the lead-up to the elections, Mobile Voter went to work with big, youth-focused organizations like World Wrestling Entertainment and Music for America. Wrestling events and concerts are ideal venues to get lots of audience members texting, and the "Smackdown" wrestlers and musicians were eager to spread the word. Voto Latino, another Mobile Voter partner, ran a successful text registration drive among Latino youth across the country. These efforts brought in tens of thousands of new voters and contributed to a record youth turnout across America in November 2006, up by around 4 percent (or more than 2 million votes) from the midterm elections of 2002.[13]

Another of the innovative organizations behind this surge in youth voting was the Bus Project, an Oregon state group founded in 2001, which has turned all its considerable creativity to making political participation quirky and fun. Its symbol is the shiny, vintage, biodiesel-fueled bus that the organizers used to bridge Oregon's urban-rural divide, sending Bus Trips of enthusiastic volunteers all over the state for voter registration and education campaigns. As you might guess from its Hip Hop Voter Drive or its "Candidates Gone Wild" debate format, the Bus Project has a particular talent for mobilizing young voters. It sponsors "Mayoraoke" events, where candidates for mayor can give a stump speech after they've sung a karaoke song. On Halloween 2004, it organized the biggest door-to-door canvass in Oregon history: Trick-or-Vote, with 800 costumed volunteers reminding Oregonians to vote in the imminent presidential elections. The Bus Project has also founded a feisty Web-based social network, Onward Oregon, to push for progressive law and policy at the state and local levels. In 2006, it registered 20,000 new voters, 83 percent of whom were young people. That's just first-time voters, and just in Oregon. If we could get a Bus Project in all fifty states, we'd bring in a whole new generation of progressive voters.

Of course, we need more than innovative ways to get more voters to the polls; we need innovative ways to counter the perennial voter suppression efforts of the other side. Sometimes that's as simple as choosing a new target. In 2006, the Secretary of State Project (SOS Project) made a groundbreaking intervention in the election of the state officials who supervise presidential election results.[14] As we all learned from Florida Secretary of State Katherine Harris in 2000 and her Ohio counterpart, Ken Blackwell, in 2004, state-level officials have the power to purge eligible voters from the rolls, exclude valid ballots, and locate precincts and voting machines in a way that greatly reduces voting in certain neighborhoods. The founders of the SOS Project realized that the best way to prevent these sorts of shenanigans was to elect a new, progressive cohort of secretaries of state (in those states where the office is directly elected).

Races for state office are relatively cheap, since candidates rarely fight it out with television advertising. By raising $500,000 for a few key campaigns and backing it up with targeted radio and cable TV ads, the SOS Project helped put five progressive candidates into the secretary of state's office in presidential swing states. In Ohio, most notably, Blackwell was succeeded by Democrat Jennifer Brunner, an election law expert who ran on a platform of protecting voters' rights. If the 2008 presidential election again hinges on Ohio, the SOS Project's early intervention might already have made all the difference.

Another strategically innovative group that made a major impact in the 2006 elections was BISC, the Ballot Initiative Strategy Center. Since the late 1970s, deep-pocketed conservative groups have frequently used ballot referendums and initiatives to get their policies passed into law. These initiatives have also become a conservative resource for mobilizing voters behind wedge issues. In California in 1994, for instance, the draconian anti-immigrant Proposition 187 carried the otherwise unpopular Republican governor, Pete Wilson, to reelection.[15] In 2004, eleven states had antigay marriage initiatives on the ballot, which were widely (if questionably) presumed to have boosted the social conservative vote for George W. Bush in swing states.[16] After decades of playing defense against better-funded conservative initiative campaigns, many weary progressive leaders had almost forgotten that direct democracy could be used by both sides.

BISC has been quietly working on this front for years, building coalitions to support progressive ballot measures and demonstrating that initiatives can be used to get out the Democratic vote as well. In 2006, BISC's work culminated in the progressive movement's first multistate, coordinated ballot initiative strategy. BISC helped get proposals to raise the minimum wage (a potential wedge issue for Democrats) onto the ballot in six states and organized progressive backing for those ballot measures. Much of the on-the-ground work to drum up support was done by progressive stalwarts such as ACORN, an advocacy group for low-income communities that has been around for thirty years, but the strategy and all-important coordination was carried out by BISC.[17]

On election day 2006, the minimum-wage initiatives won in all six states, and control of the U.S. Senate was decided by a pair of dueling ballot initiatives in Missouri. The Republicans had come up with a classic "wedge issue" initiative, prohibiting embryonic stem cell research in the state. BISC's postelection research showed that the stem cell controversy did just what it was supposed to: it "motivate[ed] conservative voters and increased the likelihood of casting their ballots for Senator Jim Talent, the Republican incumbent and vocal opponent of stem cell research." But the countervailing progressive minimum wage initiative brought out enough voters to give the Democratic candidate, Claire McCaskill, the victory.[18]

These examples show how political innovations—some technological, some tactical, and some structural—are already starting to transform progressive politics. To keep a steady stream of innovation going, we'll need flat, flexible organizational structures, not just for our movement as a whole but within and between individual progressive groups. Fortunately, the new generation of progressive organizations understands the value of decentralization and distribution of power to the grassroots.

Pillar II: Organizational Flexibility

In the wake of the 2006 elections, jubilant progressive groups all over the country organized postelection debriefings to discuss the lessons of the Democratic congressional sweep. Among all the hubbub, a seemingly eccentric new conference style stood out: the open-source "RootsCamp" debriefs sponsored by the New Organizing Institute (NOI). Each session was organized and scheduled by the participants—sometimes using a wiki Web page that any conference attendee could edit, sometimes through the less high-tech option of written notes tacked to a scheduling board. The topics of discussion were determined by the participants, not the organizers. The sessions had a "No Tourists" rule; everyone who attended was expected either to make a presentation or take part in someone else's presentation. Presentations lasted as long as they had to or until they ran into another presentation slot. It sounded like a recipe for chaos, but in practice, it produced a ferment of new ideas that will bear fruit in the 2008 election cycle.

RootsCamp is a political "unconference" model, inspired by the open-source movement in computer programming. In 2005, a group of software programmers set up the first do-it-yourself, decentralized convention in their industry, on the principle that "there was much more expertise in the audience than there possibly could be onstage." [19] The agenda at these "unconferences" is set by the people who show up. The model encourages everyone to participate as freely as possible and lets the group sift out the most valuable results from its collaboration. In the political sphere, that means not just inviting the heads of national institutions to talk at your election debrief but also integrating the invaluable local folks who might normally be sidelined: "the precinct captain, the blogger, the guerrilla ad maker . . . the head of the state party or local organization who's doing great things in a bold new way." [20]

The RootsCamp model is just one of many new techniques being promoted by the NOI, an organization dedicated to maintaining the progressive movement's early lead in online organizing. Back in the lead-up to the 2004 presidential elections, progressives enjoyed a well-publicized burst of innovation in this area. MoveOn and the Howard Dean primary campaign were the canonical examples, of course, but several other Internet-savvy Democratic organizations and campaigns also broke fund-raising and mobilization records, mainly through figuring out new ways to harness online social networks. Since 2005, the NOI has been doggedly building on this head start by training a wide range of progressive advocacy groups and candidates in cutting-edge tools of Web-based networking.

The NOI's work is exactly what we progressives need to reinforce the pillars of our political infrastructure—not only by spreading useful innovations far and wide but also by encouraging organizations to experiment with a decentralized, distributed structure. NOI Executive Director Rosalyn Lemieux explains that the goal of the organization's training seminars is to encourage just this sort of shift in strategy. "We try to make organizations more comfortable with distributing power to their supporters and letting go, in a way that allows them to grow exponentially.... They can let their would-be supporters generate the sort of content that before they would have generated. Those supporters can be their fund-raisers, can be their communication department, can even to some extent direct their political strategy."

To many progressives, it may seem obvious that decentralized networks are ideal for knowledge-based work like brainstorming, information sharing, or attacking complex problems from several sides at once. Yet even in the creative "idea generation" sector—the think tanks and strategy centers that develop and articulate the progressive agenda—young leaders can find a flat organizational structure a hard sell. Consider the experience of the Truman National Security Project.

From the Vietnam War through to the Iraq War, the Republicans have enjoyed a consistent if undeserved opinion poll lead on national security issues. The truth is, just as Democratic presidents have generally been better managers of the economy, they've also generally been better at handling foreign policy. Harry Truman, one of the strongest examples, dealt with the threats of fascism and communism through a combination of tough action, robust alliance building, and generous aid to war-torn countries. His powerful institutional legacy included NATO, the Marshall Plan, the IMF, and the World Bank. The Truman National Security Project, a strategy center founded in 2004, wants to restore the progressive movement to this sort of foreign policy leadership.

The organizational vision of the Truman Project founders was both innovative and decentralized. They would selectively identify promising young thinkers and writers on foreign policy—the progressive national security leaders of the future—and invite them to be "Truman Principals." Truman Project founder and Executive Director Rachel Kleinfeld explains that the group's main goal is to give the principals the skills, opportunities, and tools they need to succeed. "Since our inception, we have annual gatherings where the principals comment on the structure of the organization, our activities, and what they think we should be engaged in—they act like a second board. We also let them propose writings and ideas they want to work on, and if they fit with the work of the organization, we help them run with those ideas and try to get them published." Instead of starting with a detailed, centrally articulated agenda and trying to push it from the top down, the Truman Project works to identify promising young idea leaders and build them into a bottom-up movement. Ultimately, it's this sort of movement that will reclaim the national security issue for the Democrats, by creating a robust progressive foreign policy consensus and strong, intelligent messages.

While the decentralized model may seem obvious for an idea-generation group, Kleinfeld adds that it wasn't easy to get it funded and keep it going. "Even the most progressive donors don't necessarily understand the structure or the reason we do it, but we really believe that our best work comes from percolating up, not from the top down, and that it makes us a stronger, more resilient organization."

Pillar VI: Long-term Perspective

Finally, the new generation of blue political infrastructure rests solidly on the pillar of long-term vision. The leaders of these progressive organizations are focused not just on the next election but also on building ideas and institutions that will bear fruit for decades to come. We've talked about this in the context of blue financial infrastructure, but it's also a hallmark of new progressive political strategies.

One sign of this is the host of new progressive groups capitalizing on major demographic trends—in particular, the growing political significance of Americans of Hispanic descent. Hispanic Americans are already the largest minority in the United States, roughly 15 percent of the population, and are projected to grow to 25 percent of the population in another quarter century.[21] Any future-oriented progressive strategy needs to focus on winning the Hispanic vote, not only in the southwestern United States but also in the growing Spanish-speaking communities all over the country. The New Politics Institute (NPI), a think tank that grew out of the NDN strategy center in 2005, is equipping Democratic organizations to reach out to Hispanic voters. The NPI offers guidance in building up a Spanish-language communications strategy, addressing the initially daunting diversity of Hispanic groups and interests, and speaking to voters about Latin America policy. Other new progressive organizations like Voto Latino, which focus specifically on Spanish-speaking youth, will be an essential part of mobilizing the 60 percent of Hispanic Americans who are under twenty-eight years old.

Another hallmark of a long-term vision is the determination to build up state-level institutions and candidates. Nearly all national political figures emerge from state capitol buildings or governors' mansions; most of the decisions that affect our everyday lives are made at the state level; and the redistricting (or gerrymandering) that determines the course of far too many congressional races is generally carried out by state legislatures. The Republicans dominated state-level government for much of the last decade. In 2006, the Democrats decisively reversed that trend, winning 57 legislative chambers to the Republicans' 40 (with a 660-seat lead overall), plus the majority of state governorships. This victory was driven in great part by the work of new groups like Progressive Majority and Grassroots Democrats—organizations that reinforce our national movement by building at the state level.

Progressive Majority has been working since the 2004 election cycle as "the nation's only political organization dedicated exclusively to electing progressive champions at the state and local level."[22] Currently active in seven states, it recruits, supports, trains, and equips candidates for state and local races. Over three years, Progressive Majority has trained 313 candidates, of whom 196 have already gone on to win elections. Of its trainees, 140 are women and 99 are people of color (demographics where the organization carries out its most focused and determined recruiting efforts). Its achievements led *The Nation* to declare it one of the most valuable progressive groups of 2006:

> The dramatic Democratic advances in Colorado—where the party took full control of state government for the first time since John Kennedy was president—Wisconsin, Washington, Ohio and Pennsylvania were a byproduct of Progressive Majority's smart and effective grassroots approach. Indeed, Progressive Majority has been so successful in the seven states where it has operated that

party leaders and activists in other parts of the country
are clamoring for the group to come into their states.[23]

Similarly, the young 527 organization known as Grassroots
Democrats has had a major positive impact by building up the
institutional capacity of state parties. The Democratic National
Committee spent a tremendous amount of money and energy
bringing itself up to date in the late 1990s and early 2000s, but
many state-level Democratic Party organizations remained
hopelessly ill equipped for modern political communications,
online organizing, and fund-raising. Grassroots Democrats has
been working to bridge the gap, providing expertise, funding,
and networking opportunities for state party leaders. The group
helps state Democratic parties observe campaign finance law
since the dramatic changes of 2002. One reason for the weaken-
ing of state party infrastructure is that the DNC and other fed-
eral-level Democratic organizations can't raise nonfederal funds
to support their state counterparts any more. As a 527 organization, Grassroots Democrats can fill that gap.

The progressive ecosystem is not a machine; we can't take
all these new groups and slot them neatly into an old, hierarchical infrastructure. As our political capital markets continue to
nourish innovative new organizations, the landscape will
become ever more complex. In this context, as Brad deGraf of
Media Venture Collective recognizes, progressives can win by
being decentralized, by being "as different from the Republicans
as the Minutemen were from the Redcoats."[24] There's no reason
the Minutemen model can't bring about a new revolution in
American politics, with blue companies and progressive
investors mobilized behind an open, cooperative network of
organizations and activists.

CHAPTER 10

Blue America

The Future Progressive Majority

WE BEGAN THIS BOOK WITH A PROMISE TO SHOW that progressive values are better than the irresponsible right-wing alternative—not just morally better but better for business. The success of the Blue Sector is powerful evidence that nice guys do finish first, that progressive investors and companies can both make money and make a real difference in the world. Yet despite its market-tested record of success, the Blue Sector is still a minority phenomenon. As we've seen, if the S&P 500 were a democracy, it would be more monolithically Republican than the American government at the height of George W. Bush and Tom DeLay's power.

In the market, of course, it doesn't really matter that progressive companies are outnumbered five to one, as long as their stock continues to outperform their competitors' by such a striking margin. Companies are not created equal, and business success isn't decided by majority vote. In fact, companies can even benefit from being members of a distinct, successful minority, thanks to investors' desire to whittle down the intimidating breadth of the market into a smaller, more manageable set of high-return investments.

In politics, though, progressives have also found themselves in the minority for much of the past quarter century—and in Washington, unlike on Wall Street, minorities don't have many chances to outperform the majority. After conservatives took over the presidency, the Supreme Court, the Congress, and most state governorships and legislatures, plenty of people took Karl Rove seriously when he talked about a permanent Republican majority. The disarray in the progressive movement after we lost control of Congress only exacerbated the problem. Plenty of pundits began describing the Democrats as a party of the two coasts and not much else (with a definition of "the coasts" that stopped at Virginia in the east and excluded major Republican oases in California).

Of course, a lot fewer people have been talking about a permanent Republican majority since November 2006, but you'll still hear a lot of people argue that "the Democrats didn't win the election, the Republicans lost it." The underlying assumption is that a progressive manifesto can't win majority support unless the other side undergoes a dramatic meltdown. Does the success of the Blue Sector really hold out the promise of a broader progressive revival, or are blue companies, organizations, and political parties destined to remain a minority in an overwhelmingly red arena?

Myth: The progressive movement doesn't speak for a majority of Americans.

If the Powell Memorandum and the Republican machine show us anything, it's that there's no such thing as a permanent or natural majority party. The conservative majority was built through hard work, visionary ideas, innovative institutions, and (not least) deep, liquid political capital markets. We have to respect what the right wing has achieved over the last three decades, but we shouldn't be intimidated by it. Echoing the spirit of Lewis Powell's manifesto, we say, We can achieve everything they've achieved, and we can do it even better.

Progressives have had an uphill fight since the conservative ascendancy began, and we haven't always been marching in the right direction. As long as we enjoyed a Democratic congressional majority, it was easy to underestimate the threat from the right wing, and it took us a while to regroup after losing Congress. Only in the last few years have we begun putting into place the capital markets, innovative political tools, and decentralized networks that we'll need to win back a majority. Fortunately, this progressive awakening comes at the same time that the Republican model of business and politics is collapsing under the weight of corruption scandals and mismanagement.

We agree with Simon Rosenberg, founder of NDN and the New Politics Institute, that we have just passed a significant turning point: "The basic narrative of the last generation of American politics . . . has been the assumption that conservative ideology was ascendant and ours was in decline. That narrative ended in November 2006. We're now looking at an equal playing field, which is a very exciting place to be. The Republicans are on a downward trend, the Democrats are on an upward trend. Right now, it's up for grabs."

> **Reality: The generation of conservative dominance is over. The coming decade will see a progressive revival in American politics, business, and society, based on the values and principles of progressive leadership.**

A couple of years ago, it made sense to speculate about a permanent Republican majority and to wonder whether Democrats were slipping into irrelevance. The Gallup Poll regularly tracks "party identification," asking Americans every year whether they identify themselves as Republicans, Democrats, or independents. Historically, Democrats have enjoyed an advantage on this front; the Republicans won elections not because they spoke for more Americans but because they reliably got more of their constituents to the polls while suppressing the Democratic vote. In 2002, however, the Democrats lost their lead in party identification. For three years, more Americans identified themselves as Republicans than Democrats. In 2004, for the first time, self-identified Republicans passed independents too, becoming at 34.2 percent the largest self-identified political bloc in the country.[1] Combined with George W. Bush's narrow election victory and the continued Republican control of Congress, many jubilant conservatives declared that this showed a permanent shift of attitude in their favor. Gloomy progressive pundits speculated that the September 11, 2001, attacks might have created a major realignment in American politics, as voters identified themselves with the party of the president and believed George W. Bush's promise of national security.

Today, it is clear just how thoroughly the Republicans squandered their opportunity. In 2005, as the Bush administration was losing its way over Iraq, Hurricane Katrina, and Social Security, the Democrats regained the advantage in party identification. By 2006, a robust 34.3 percent of Gallup's respondents said they identified themselves as Democrats—and when you threw in independents who said they lean Democratic, the total rose to 50.4 percent, the first time any party has passed the 50 percent mark since Gallup started polling on independent "leanings" sixteen years ago. The same 2006 poll found that thirty-three states were currently leaning Democratic—including former Republican strongholds such as Arizona, Oklahoma, and Virginia—compared to only six states where Republicans had a clear advantage. Nine states that had leaned strongly Republican for years were up for grabs in 2006, including Alabama, Kansas, and Montana.[2] Of course, that translated into an electoral landslide, with Democratic candidates winning all across the country.

This doesn't mean that we Democrats can declare ourselves a majority party and rest on our laurels. We have a window of opportunity, just as the Republicans had after 9/11. We might squander it as they did. But the 2006 elections should at least lay to rest the idea that Democrats are inherently a minority party. Our core progressive values of fair play, environmental sustainability, equal opportunity, and good governance spoke powerfully to voters all over the country. Culture war issues like gay rights and abortion failed to drown out the appeal of straight-talking red state candidates like Jon Tester in Montana and Jim Webb in Virginia. Issues like an increased minimum wage and better health care galvanized voters from Stockton, California, to Black Mountain, North Carolina. We won back the Hispanic voters and women who had leaned toward George W. Bush in 2004. With the GOP's lock on government broken, we now have a chance to reclaim the political center—and that doesn't mean meeting the Republicans way over on the right where they've dragged our national political discourse. It means pulling the center back to the experience of ordinary, hardworking Americans and pushing forward with courageous leadership on key social and environmental issues.

If Democrats are to speak for a majority of Americans, we believe they must complete their thirty-year transition from a hierarchical party to a decentralized one, making full use of the latest technologies and organizational tactics to empower the progressive grass roots. The Democratic Party is starting to understand itself as one key element in a thriving political network. We are building a generation of catalytic leaders who understand the paradox that you can gain power by letting it go. By distributing power to the local level, we benefit tremendously in growth, creativity, and commitment. We need to be aware of what we're doing if we're going to pull it off, and to invest in organizations that have the know-how to help us get there.

We also need to put more time and energy into refining our progressive political capital markets. A thriving, open market lets the best political investors find the best political entrepreneurs and ensures that a wider variety of ideas make it to fruition. As Simon Rosenberg of NDN points out, "Once you've built a robust capital market, you can be less worried about funding toward a strategy," because the movement will have a deep enough pool of investors to take risks, make mistakes, and support the unanticipated innovations that change the game. We've taken the first steps by bringing large and small investors alike into a flexible financial infrastructure, as the Republicans did decades ago. Now we need to deepen the aquifer. We need more capital; more grass-roots-driven small-donor fund-raising; more progressive foundations that are willing to back explicitly political causes. We need a continuing stream of innovations like the NPC's "mutual funds" and ActBlue's empowerment of individual fund-raisers.

Profit and Politics

The Blue Sector will be an essential source of capital and private-sector insights for the progressive revival. Our political infrastructure faces major tests every two to four years; blue companies are tested every day. The progressive movement can learn from ongoing blue company experiments in areas such as organizational structure and investing in employees. The Blue Sector will also bring an essential voice to the continuing progressive debate over how to create a more just, sustainable, and equitable world. The progressive mission should not be just to keep irresponsible corporations from doing damage but also to encourage more companies to profit by making the world a better place. We can harness corporate power, not just curb it.

In American politics, we foresee the time when donors may blur the traditional line between for-profit companies and nonprofit organizations. If the Blue Sector proves anything, it's that there's no contradiction between building a better world and making money. Plenty of successful corporate leaders understand this already. A new crop of "philanthropreneurs" are dedicating their humanitarian money to for-profit ventures that have major social and environmental benefits.[3] Richard Branson of Virgin Group has committed the profits from Virgin's train and airline businesses (an estimated $3 billion over the next ten years) to fighting climate change, mainly through the development of profitable alternative fuels. Pierre Omidyar, a founder of eBay, has contributed greatly to international microfinance groups that extend affordable credit to the world's poor and help them become entrepreneurs. Google's philanthropic foundation has given its largest single grant ($5 million) to the venture capital Acumen Fund. Though both the Google Foundation and Acumen are nonprofit organizations, Acumen is dedicated to supporting profit-making solutions to developing-country problems, such as "low-cost mortgages in Pakistan and rural health clinics in Kenya" and "affordable private ambulances in India."[4]

Similarly, over the next decade progressive investors and entrepreneurs will be able to profit from new political media platforms, including radio, cable, and digital media channels. We predict that the most fascinating (and in some ways troubling) blend of politics with business will be a new generation of "digital lifestyle" tools. As the Internet moves decisively onto the average American's cell phone or handheld media player, it's going to open up a new world of political marketing—not the intrusive broadcast marketing of the television age, but the subtler sort of ads we get on the margins of Google and Amazon, narrowly targeted to the lifestyle and consumer preferences of the individual user. Imagine a future version of alonovo.com or BuyBlue.org that lets us shop only at companies that meet our personal criteria for political and social responsibility. The program will also allow companies to refine their marketing to the same level of precision, shaping their products and policies to individual consumer demand. Americans will see a whole new consumer world adapted to their personal values. For progressives, that will mean "No child labor used to make these running shoes." "Union made." "100 percent recycled content." "Earth tones worn by Al Gore." "Barack Obama's favorite album." "Official cowboy hats of the Dixie Chicks." And "This company sends 10 percent of its pretax profits to Democratic candidates."

As broadcast media shrink in popularity, individual lifestyle choices will become the basis of advertising; we'll increasingly see only the ads that interest us personally. On the flip side, all the goods and services we buy and all the entertainment we enjoy will come with subtle messages that cater to and reinforce our preexisting convictions. Companies won't be limited by the fear of antagonizing everyone else who sees the ad, since it's targeted to the views of an individual consumer. This new marketing will shape our offline lifestyle by steering us to music, books, shops, restaurants, vacations, friends, and (not least) political candidates. If we progressives recognize that this shift is coming, we can capitalize on it both politically and financially, while also preparing to address the potentially alarming aspects of the digital lifestyle revolution: the privacy issues, the deepened entanglement of big companies in politics, the increased difficulty of getting a message across to anyone who doesn't already want to hear it.

Blue and Bluer

Some readers might be wondering what a long-term American progressive revival would do to the Blue Sector. What would happen if blue companies grew from around 15 percent of the S&P 500 to 50 percent or even more? Is it likely that American business will at some future point accept a blue agenda?

As of this writing, it isn't clear how the market will respond to the change in the political winds. We can certainly expect the number of red companies to shrink over the next year or two, if only because Republican leaders no longer command the sticks and carrots they wielded so freely to keep the PAC contributions rolling in. Since the Democrats reclaimed Congress, we've already seen some corporations and lobbyists trying to make up for years of overinvestment in the GOP. We don't expect the new Congress to be either as bullying or as lobbyist-friendly as its predecessor, so there probably won't be a wholesale shift of companies into the Democratic camp. It would also take a while for most companies to "go blue" by our standards; ten years of enthusiastically funding the GOP don't balance out quickly. But we do envision a growing number of big companies giving blue and hopefully even acting blue—especially as word gets out about the power of genuinely progressive behavior.

Here's what we see happening as more companies embrace the principles of progressive leadership. First, the United States will enjoy greater prosperity and sustainable success. We don't see any reason why progressive behavior would be less rewarding (in absolute terms) if more companies started engaging in it. Second, the political role of business will return to a balance it hasn't seen since the time of the Powell Memorandum. In fact, we suspect that red companies and even the Republican Party will be pulled toward a centrist or even slightly progressive set of values. As the bankruptcy of the old conservative model becomes ever clearer, they'll follow the money—and the money will be in corporate social responsibility, in good corporate governance, in respectful treatment of workers and the environment.

Third, the companies that are *most* committed to progressive values will continue to outperform the rest of the pack. Investors need not despair at the prospect of a diluted Blue Index. It's true that the relative performance of the Blue Sector would almost certainly be less impressive if it grew to 50 percent or more of the S&P 500. That's just simple mathematics; as a class of companies grows in proportion to the market as a whole, it is less likely to perform above average.

But we believe that a more demanding standard for "acting blue" would identify a smaller set of even more committed, even more successful companies. In setting up the Blue Index, we allowed for a three-strike system; a company can survive receiving one or two negative marks in KLD's social responsibility analysis before we count it as nonblue. We wanted to encourage investors to engage with big companies that generally accept progressive values but occasionally need a push in the right direction. We also wanted to encourage as many companies as possible to think of themselves as blue and start perceiving their own success as an outgrowth of their (often imperfect) progressive behavior.

What would happen if we switched to a two-strike standard? The seventy-six current constituents of the Blue Index have outperformed the S&P 500 by 19.43 percent over the last five years. If we were to impose a two-strike rule for "acting blue," the Blue Index would shrink to fifty-three companies, which have beaten the S&P 500 over five years by 21.24 percent. In other words, the more socially responsible blue companies are (by and large), the more financially successful they are as well.

As corporate America shifts in a more progressive direction, the bluest companies will widen their advantage. Right now, "giving blue" is the strongest single indicator of successful companies. If more companies begin giving money to the Democrats simply because the Democrats are the party in power and not out of a genuine commitment to progressive values, "acting blue" will become a less powerful differentiating factor. No matter what, blue investment will still be a way to both get rich and make the world a better place.

Finally, we believe that the expansion of the Blue Sector will have a positive global impact. Innovative, progressive corporations can play a constructive role in many thorny international dilemmas, from climate change to sustainable poverty relief. As a recent article in the *Stanford Social Innovation Review* pointed out, "The world's problems do not neatly apportion themselves between the private, nonprofit, and public sectors. Many of our most pressing challenges—economic development, job training, housing, medical research, and the logistics of disaster or famine relief—are rooted in circumstances where businesses have deep expertise that nonprofits and governments lack."[5] Companies like Nike and Gap have already thrown themselves wholeheartedly into the problem of improving global labor conditions. If even one of the big American energy companies became consistently blue and channeled its colossal profits into a serious program of clean energy research, just imagine the impact that could have on the world's climate.

America's blue companies are also in a position to transform the philosophy of business around the world. In Europe, corporate social responsibility is already popular among business leaders. European skeptics, however, point to supposedly irresponsible America (and the writings of conservative American analysts) as evidence that companies don't need to be socially responsible to get ahead. The Blue Sector can be an ally to the most ethical European companies, reaffirming their commitment to making the world a better place. In emerging markets, where many of the rising corporations look to America for partners, rivals, and exemplars, the Blue Way could have an even greater impact. What would happen in the rising markets of

China and India if the newly global, fast-growing corporations there come to understand the pillars of progressive leadership?

Some of them have already figured it out, like Ratan Tata, chairman of India's enormous Tata Group. Since he took over in 1991, the septuagenarian chairman has led his family's conglomerate to international success, including the daring 2007 acquisition of the Anglo-Dutch steelmaker Corus by Tata Steel. A recent profile in *The Economist* revealed that Tata's business strategy has been shaped by some familiar-sounding values. "He does not seem to be motivated by money, and talks constantly about fairness and doing the right thing. 'I want to be able to go to bed at night and say that I haven't hurt anybody,' Mr Tata says twice in the course of an interview. . . . Two-thirds of Tata Sons is owned by charitable trusts that do good works in India, and the firm is known for refusing to pay bribes and for treating workers well."[6] We suspect that if Ratan Tata worked in America, he would be running a blue company.

The Blue Way is, literally, about investing in a better world. The alliance among progressive investors, citizens, companies, and political organizations in America will not only benefit those of us who participate in it directly; it will also make our nation more prosperous and just. It will transform and revive the Democratic Party. It will improve labor conditions and the environment around the globe. And it will provide a progressive model of capitalism for other countries. For all of us who are genuinely invested in a vision of global justice, freedom, and sustainability, the Blue Way is the way forward.

Notes

1. THE GREAT ILLUSION

1. Market-cap-weighted average share price of blue companies in the S&P 500 compared to the 500 current constituents of the S&P 500, July 2001 to July 2006. Blue Investment Management analysis, using data from Morningstar and the Center for Responsive Politics (www.opensecrets.org) as of March 1, 2007.

2. SEEING RED

1. MediaMatters for America, "ABC Memo Reveals Air America Advertiser Blacklist," October 31, 2006 (mediamatters.org/items/200610310008).
2. John B. Judis, *The Paradox of American Democracy* (Routledge Press, 2001), p. 109.
3. P. B. Gray, "Inside the Chamber," *CFO Magazine,* June 1, 2006.
4. "2004 Cycle Large Donors to PoliticalMoneyLine's Key 527 Groups," PoliticalMoneyLine (www.fecinfo.com/cgi-win/irs_ef_527.exe?DoFn=&sYR=2004).
5. "IRS 527 Filers, 2006 Cycle and 2004 Cycle," PoliticalMoneyLine (www.fecinfo.com).
6. Blue Investment Management analysis using data from the Center for Responsive Politics (www.opensecrets.org) as of Decem-

ber 31, 2006. "Neutral" companies either give equally to both parties or make no formal political contributions at all.

7. Blue Investment Management analysis using data from the Center for Responsive Politics (www.opensecrets.org) as of December 31, 2006.

8. Blue Investment Management analysis using data from the Center for Responsive Politics (www.opensecrets.org) as of December 31, 2006.

9. Blue Investment Management analysis using data from the Center for Responsive Politics (www.opensecrets.org) as of December 31, 2006.

10. The National Committee for Responsive Philanthropy, "The Waltons and Wal-Mart: Self-Interested Philanthropy," October 4, 2005.

11. Center for Responsive Politics (www.opensecrets.org/lobbyists/index.asp) as of December 31, 2006

12. The K Street Project now has a Web site: www.kstreetproject.com. Its impact on Washington has been well chronicled by Nicholas Confessore in "Welcome to the Machine," *Washington Monthly,* July–August 2003, www.washingtonmonthly.com/features/2003/0307.confessore.html. See also Elizabeth Drew, "Selling Washington," *The New York Review of Books,* 52, no. 11 (June 23, 2005), and Sheldon Rampton and John Stauber, *Banana Republicans* (New York: Jeremy P. Tarcher/Penguin, 2004), pp. 102–107.

13. See Drew, "Selling Washington."

14. Bob Cusack, "Big Insurer Lost Its Bet on the Dems," *The Hill,* November 24, 2004 (www.thehill.com/news/11242004/insurer.aspx).

15. Center for Responsive Politics (www.opensecrets.org).

16. Center for Responsive Politics (www.opensecrets.org/news/enron/enron_other.asp) as of December 31, 2006.

17. Center for Responsive Politics (www.opensecrets.org/industries/indus.asp?Ind=F07) as of December 31, 2006.

18. See Confessore, "Welcome to the Machine."

19. Trisha Brick, "Investing in Social Change." *FOCUS,* Boston University School of Theology, Winter 2005–2006 (www.bu.edu/sth/

focus/2006/tyson/index.html). The origins of Pax World Funds are also summed up briefly on the Pax World Web site at www .paxworld.com/02_history.htm.

20. Lewis Powell, "Attack on American Free Enterprise System," U.S. Chamber of Commerce Confidential Memorandum, August 24, 1971. The text of the Powell Memorandum is available online courtesy of MediaTransparency.org (www.mediatransparency.org/ story.php?storyID=22), along with a thorough analysis by Jerry Landay, "The Attack Memo That Changed America: The Powell Manifesto," August 20, 2002 (www.mediatransparency.org/story. php?storyID=21).

21. Landay, "Attack Memo." The role of the Powell Memorandum in spurring Joseph Coors to fund the Heritage Foundation is also made clear in Lee Edwards, *The Power of Ideas: The Heritage Foundation at 25 Years* (Ottawa, Ill.: Jameson Books, 1997), chapter 1, p. 9.

22. Judis, *The Paradox of American Democracy,* p. 120.

23. Ibid., p. 131, citing Sar A. Levitan and Martha R. Cooper, *Business Lobbies: The Public Good and the Bottom Line* (Baltimore: Johns Hopkins University Press, 1983).

24. Center for Responsive Politics (www.opensecrets.org/lobbyists/ index.asp) as of December 31, 2006.

25. Social Investment Forum, *2005 Report on Socially Responsible Investing Trends in the United States—10 Year Review,* January 24, 2006 (www.socialinvest.org/areas/research/trends/sri_trends_ report_2005.pdf), p. v.

26. Ibid., p. 7.

27. Ibid., pp. iv, 7, 56–57.

28. Joseph F. Keefe, "Should Socially Responsible Investing Be More "Political"? A Blue Growth Strategy for a Green Industry," unpublished paper, 2006.

29. "A Halo for Angel Investors: A Portfolio of Investments in Socially Responsible Companies Can Generate Returns Similar to Those of the S&P 500," McKinsey Quarterly no. 1 (2004).

30. Marc Orlitzky, Frank L. Schmidt, and Sara L. Rynes, "Corporate Social and Financial Performance: A Meta-analysis." *Organization Studies,* 24, 2003.

31. See, e.g., Jeroen Derwall et al., "The Eco-Efficiency Premium Puzzle," *Financial Analysts Journal,* March–April 2005, 51–63.

32. Blue Investment Management analysis using publicly available returns data from Morningstar as of June 1, 2007.

33. David Vogel, *The Market for Virtue* (Washington, D.C.: Brookings Institution Press, 2005).

34. Blue Investment Management analysis using publicly available returns data from Google Finance as of June 1, 2007.

35. World Economic Forum, "Trust Survey Results," December 15, 2005.

3. BEING BLUE PUTS COMPANIES IN THE BLACK

1. "More Pain than Gain," *The Economist,* September 14, 2006.

2. "Bush Signs Repeal of Ergonomic Rules into Law," CNN, March 20, 2001 (http://archives.cnn.com/2001/ALLPOLITICS/03/20/bush.ergonomics/).

3. "8 Million May Lose OT Pay," CNN, June 27, 2003 (http://.money.cnn.com/2003/06/26/news/economy/epi, cited in David Sirota, Hostile Takeover [New York: Crown Publishing, 2006], p. 56).

4. See Sirota, *Hostile Takeover,* pp. 107–108.

5. See *State of New York, et al. v. Environmental Protection Agency,* 443 F.3d 880 (D.C. Cir. 2006) (http://pacer.cadc.uscourts.gov/docs/common/opinions/200603/03-1380a.pdf).

6. PWC Global CEO Survey 2003.

7. Tara Weiss, "New Lessons In Corporate Citizenship," *Forbes,* November 28, 2006.

8. Ed Crooks and Sheila McNulty, "Exxon Reports Largest Profit in US History," *Financial Times,* February 1, 2007.

9. Blue Investment Management, using data from opensecrets.org as of December 31, 2006.

10. Blue Investment Management, using data from opensecrets.org and KLD Analytics as of December 31, 2006.

11. "The BusinessWeek 50" is an annual feature of *BusinessWeek* magazine, available online at www.businessweek.com.

12. Test was carried out in July 2006, for the previous five years from June 2001 to June 2006. The margin of error was 0.0003.

13. Blue Investment Management analysis, using publicly available company and sector performance data from Morningstar as of November 16, 2006.

14. National Association of Real Estate Investment Trusts.

15. In the 2002 and 2004 election cycles, oil and gas companies gave 80 percent of their donations to Republicans. In the 2006 cycle to date, they have given 83 percent of their donations to Republicans. Data from Center for Responsive Politics, October 23, 2006 (www.opensecrets.org/industries/indus.asp?Ind=E01).

16. Blue Investment Management Analysis using publicly available data from Google Finance and Morningstar as of June 1, 2007.

17. Michael J. Cooper, Huseyin Gulen, and Alexei V. Ovtchinnikov, "Corporate Political Contributions and Stock Returns," January 23, 2007 (http://ssrn.com/abstract=940790).

18. Ibid., p. 16.

19. Ibid., p. 5.

20. Michael Brush, "Why Politicians Are Worth Buying," *MSN Money,* February 7, 2007 (articles.moneycentral.msn.com/Invest ing/CompanyFocus/WhyPoliticiansAreWorthBuying.aspx).

21. John O'Donnell, "The RPSEA Rip-off: How the Natural Gas Industry Extracted a Billion-Dollar Boondoggle from Congress," Public Citizen, January 2007 (www.cleanupwashington.org/docu ments/RPSEAreport.pdf).

22. Ronald Brownstein, "Republicans Run the Political Risk of Becoming Too Self-Reliant," Los Angeles Times, August 8, 2005.

4. THE PRINCIPLES OF PROGRESSIVE LEADERSHIP I

1. Jessie Scanlon, "How to Turn Money Into Innovation," *Business-Week,* November 14, 2006.
2. All corporate political contribution breakdowns in this chapter have been calculated by Blue Investment Management using data from the Center for Responsive Politics (www.opensecrets.org) as of December 31, 2006. All comparisons between blue company share price performance and the S&P 500 are based on data from Morningstar as of June 1, 2007.
3. "America's Most Admired Companies 2006: Best & Worst: Inno-vation," *Fortune* (http://money.cnn.com/magazines/fortune/most admired/best_worst/best1.html).
4. Scanlon, "How to Turn Money into Innovation."
5. Peter Burrows et al., "Steve Jobs' Magic Kingdom," *Business-Week,* February 6, 2006.
6. Peter Burrows, "Byte of the Apple: How Can Apple Be Worth More than Dell?" *BusinessWeek,* January 20, 2006.
7. National Association of Real Estate Investment Trusts.
8. Mark David, "Big Brother in the Back Seat: TripSense Records Your Ride," *Electronic Design,* September 6, 2004. See also Pro-gressive Auto Insurance, U.S. Patent 5,797,134, "Motor Vehicle Monitoring System for Determining a Cost of Insurance," August 18, 1998.
9. Eric Wahlgren, "Has Progressive Gotten Ahead of Itself?" *Busi-nessWeek,* April 5, 2004.
10. See David Shook, "Forest Labs: Feeling No Pain," *BusinessWeek,* March 23, 2003; Scanlon, "How to Turn Money into Innovation."
11. Ori Brafman and Rod A. Beckstrom, *The Starfish and the Spider* (New York: Portfolio, 2006).
12. Ibid., p. 81.
13. Quentin Hardy, "Google Thinks Small," *Forbes,* November 14, 2005.
14. Hardy, "Google Thinks Small."

15. Lindsay Gerdes, "They Love It Here, and Here, and Here," *BusinessWeek,* June 4, 2006.

16. Charles Fishman, "The Anarchist's Cookbook," *Fast Company,* 84, July 2004, p. 70.

17. Ibid.

18. Ryan Underwood, "Employee Innovator Runner-up: Whole Foods Market," *Fast Company,* issue 99, October 2005, p. 58.

19. Fishman, "The Anarchist's Cookbook."

20. Nanette Byrnes, "What's Beyond for Bed Bath & Beyond?" *BusinessWeek,* January 19, 2004.

21. Marcia Stepanek, "Q&A with Progressive's Peter Lewis," *BusinessWeek,* September 12, 2000.

22. Jeroen Derwall et al., "The Eco-efficiency Premium Puzzle," *Financial Analysts Journal,* March–April 2005.

23. See Derwall et al.; Herbert D. Blank and C. Michael Carty, "The Eco-efficiency Anomaly," Innovest Working Paper, June 2002 (www.innovestgroup.com/pdfs/Eco_Anomaly_7_02.pdf); Nadia Guenster et al., "The Economic Value of Corporate Eco-Efficiency," Working Paper, Erasmus University, July 25, 2005 (www .abo.fi/fak/esf/fei/redovisa/kurser/Dorpat/Guenster percent20wppercent202005.pdf).

24. See Abby Joseph Cohen, "Capital Markets at the Crossroads: Sustainable Investing: Environmental Focus," prepared by Goldman Sachs & Co. for the Clinton Global Initiative Annual Meeting, September 2006.

25. William McDonough and Michael Braungart, "From Inspiration to Innovation," *green@work,* July–August 2002.

26. Andrew T. Gillies, "Cradle to Cradle to Washington," *Forbes,* December 15, 2004.

27. McDonough and Braungart, "From Inspiration to Innovation."

28. Stanley Holmes, "Nike Goes for the Green," *BusinessWeek,* September 25, 2006.

29. Joann Muller, "Control Freaks," *Forbes,* January 8, 2007; Marjorie

Kelly, "100 Best Corporate Citizens for 2006," *Business Ethics,* 20 no. 1 (Spring 2006).

30. Katie Sosnowchik, "Less Is More," *green@work,* May–June 2004.
31. Muller, "Control Freaks."
32. Information from KLD Research & Analytics report on Johnson Controls, "Pollution Prevention Strength Commentary" section, as of January 11, 2007.
33. Sosnowchik, "Less Is More."
34. "Johnson Controls to Receive 2004 World Environment Center Gold Medal for International Corporate Achievement in Sustainable Development," World Environment Center press release, January 15, 2004 (www.wec.org/news.php?id=12).
35. "Fiscal 2006 Fast Facts," Johnson Controls (www.johnsoncontrols.com/corp_profile/corp_profile.htm).
36. Sarah Gardener, "Quest for the Holy Grail of Coffee Cups," Marketplace, American Public Media, July 14, 2006.
37. "Starbucks Environmental Leadership Drives Industry First with Use of the Only FDA Approved Recycled-Content Cup," *E-Wire,* November 11, 2004.
38. See May 2002 Innovest report on FPL Energy (www.innovestgroup.com/pdfs/FPL_0502.pdf).
39. "Whole Foods Goes with the Wind," *USA Today,* January 9, 2006.
40. Kathryn Balint, "Qualcomm Praised for Taking the Work Out of Getting to Work," *San Diego Union-Tribune,* October 20, 2005.

5. THE PRINCIPLES OF PROGRESSIVE LEADERSHIP II

1. Powell, "Attack" (www.mediatransparency.org/story.php?storyID=22).
2. David Sirota, *Hostile Takeover* (New York: Crown Publishing, 2006), p. 71.
3. "McJob, n." *Oxford English Dictionary* (Oxford University Press, 1998).
4. Patricia O'Connell, "A Full-Bodied Talk with Mr. Starbucks,"

BusinessWeek, October 2004; "Face Value: Staying Pure," *The Economist,* February 23, 2006.

5. O'Connell, "Full-Bodied."

6. "Starbucks Coffee Company," Case Study No. 1-0023, Tuck School of Business at Dartmouth College, 2002, (http://mba.tuck.dartmouth.edu/pdf/2002-1-0023.pdf), p. 4.

7. Steven Greenhouse, "How Costco Became the Anti-Wal-Mart," *The New York Times,* July 17, 2005.

8. Ibid.

9. Julie Schmit, "Costco Wins Loyalty with Bulky Bargains," *USA Today,* September 23, 2004.

10. Greenhouse, "How Costco Became."

11. "Study Finds Wal-Mart Contributes to Poverty," *St. Louis Business Journal,* May 17, 2006.

12. Schmit, "Costco Wins Loyalty."

13. Stanley Holmes and Wendy Zellner, "The Costco Way," *BusinessWeek,* April 12, 2004.

14. Richard Dunham, "A Mutual Fund That Plays Politics," *BusinessWeek,* February 5, 2007.

15. Fred Kaplan, "Sidney Harman," *Regardies,* September 1989.

16. Bill Barker, "The Best Stocks of the Millennium," Motley Fool, November 20, 2006 (www.fool.com/investing/small-cap/2006/11/20/the-best-stocks-of-the-millennium.aspx).

17. Adam Lashinsky, "Working in the Googleplex: Spin Doctors," *Fortune,* January 8, 2007.

18. *Fortune*'s "100 Best Companies to Work For: 2007" report is available online at money.cnn.com/magazines/fortune/bestcompanies/2007.

19. *Fortune,* "100 Best Companies to Work For: 2007."

20. Hannah Clark, "Whole Foods: Spinning CEO Pay," *Forbes,* April 20, 2006.

21. Naomi Klein, "Bush to NGOs: Watch Your Mouths," *The Globe and Mail* (Toronto), June 20, 2003.

22. For the example of Nike, see Mark Kramer and John Kania,

"Changing the Game: Leading Corporations Switch from Defense to Offense in Solving Global Problems," *Stanford Social Innovation Review,* Spring 2006, pp. 26–27.

23. Aaron Bernstein, Michael Shari, and Elisabeth Malkin, "A World of Sweatshops," *BusinessWeek,* November 6, 2000.

24. Nike's "FY 04 Corporate Responsibility Report," April 13, 2005, is available online at www.nike.com/nikebiz/nikebiz.jhtml?page=29&item=fy04; Gap Inc.'s "Facing Challenges, Finding Opportunities: 2004 Social Responsibility Report," July 13, 2005, is available online at www.gapinc.com/public/documents/CSR_Report_04.pdf.

25. "100 Best Corporate Citizens for 2006," *Business Ethics Magazine,* 20, no. 1 (Spring 2006). Nike is at number 13 and Gap Inc. at number 21.

26. The annual Ceres-ACCA Sustainability Reporting Awards are available online at www.ceres.org/sustreporting/reporting_awards.php.

27. SustainAbility Ltd., "Tomorrow's Value: The Global Reporters 2006 Survey of Corporate Sustainability Reporting," November 2006, available online at www.sustainability.com/insight/research-article.asp?id=458.

28. Michael Connor, "Getting Engaged," *CRO Magazine,* Fall 2006 (www.thecro.com/?q=node/1).

29. Dexter Roberts and Pete Engardio, "Secrets, Lies, and Sweatshops," *BusinessWeek,* November 27, 2006.

30. Felicity Barringer, "A Coalition for Firm Limit on Emissions," *The New York Times,* January 19, 2007.

31. David R. Baker, "Pocket Change to Change the World," *San Francisco Chronicle,* December 19, 2006.

32. Timothy Gardner, "Exxon Meets Green Groups as Climate Focus Surges," Reuters, January 13, 2007.

33. "Frequently Asked Questions: What Is Starbucks' Role in Fair Trade?" TransFair USA (http://transfairusa.org/content/resources/faq-advanced.php).

34. Kerry Howley, "Absolution in Your Cup: The Real Meaning of Fair Trade Coffee," *Reason,* March 2006.

35. Starbucks, "Corporate Social Responsibility: 2005 Annual Report" (www.starbucks.com/aboutus/csrannualreport.asp).

36. Nanette Byrnes, "What's Beyond for Bed Bath & Beyond?" *BusinessWeek,* January 19, 2004.

37. Alan B. Goldberg and Bill Ritter,"Costco CEO Finds Pro-Worker Means Profitability," ABC News, December 2, 2005.

38. John Mackey, "Conscious Capitalism: Creating a New Paradigm for Business," November 2006 (www.wholefoods.com/blogs/jm/archives/2006/11/conscious_capit.html).

6. BUY BLUE

1. A. Q. Mowbray, *The Thumb on the Scale; Or the Supermarket Shell Game* (Philadelphia: Lippincott, 1967).

2. Kathryn Kish Sklar, *Florence Kelley and the Nation's Work* (New Haven: Yale University Press, 1995).

3. Patty Freeman Evans, "U.S. Online Retail Forecast, 2005 to 2010," JupiterResearch, February 2006, confirmed by "Quarterly Retail E-Commerce Sales, 2nd Quarter 2006," U.S. Census Bureau News, August 17, 2006 (www.census.gov/mrts/www/data/pdf/06Q2.pdf).

4. Evans, "U.S. Online Retail Forecast, 2005 to 2010."

5. Former BuyBlue.org research director Martha Ture, quoted in "Companies in the Crossfire," *BusinessWeek,* April 17, 2006.

6. "Companies in the Crossfire," *BusinessWeek,* April 17, 2006.

7. Blue Investment Management, using data from www.opensecrets.org, as of November 16, 2006.

8. Wil S. Hyton, "Not Necessarily the News," *GQ,* November 21, 2005 (men.style.com/gq/features/landing?id=content_4024).

9. Eric Boehlert, "No Pundit Left Behind," Salon.com, January 12, 2005.

10. Eric Klinenberg, "Beyond Fair & Balanced," Rolling Stone, February 10, 2005 (www.rollingstone.com/politics/story/6959139/beyond_fair_and_balanced/).

11. "Department of Education—Contract to Obtain Services of Arm-

strong Williams," Government Accountability Office (GAO), September 30, 2005 (www.gao.gov/decisions/appro/305368.pdf).

12. Terence Smith, "News or Views?" PBS, October 12, 2004 (www.pbs.org/newshour/bb/media/july-dec04/sinclair_10-12.html).

13. Eric Boehlert, "Sinclair's Disgrace," Salon.com, October 14, 2004.

14. Hyton, "Not Necessarily the News"; "Sinclair Drops Plan to Air Full Anti-Kerry Film," Media Matters for America, mediamatters .org/items/200410200001.

15. The RED Campaign Web site is www.joinred.com.

16. Apple press release, November 3, 2006 (www.apple.com/pr/library/2006/nov/03nano.html).

17. The history of the Church of Stop Shopping is available at www.revbilly.com.

7. PAINTING WALL STREET BLUE

1. "Shareholder Democracy: Battling for Corporate America," *The Economist,* March 9, 2006.

2. For a further discussion, see Robert Monks, Anthony Miller, and Jacqueline Cook, "Shareholder Activism on Environmental Issues," *Natural Resources Forum* 28, no. 4 (November 2004), p. 319.

3. Social Investment Forum, *2005 Report on Socially Responsible Investing Trends in the United States—10 Year Review,* January 24, 2006 (www.socialinvest.org/areas/research/trends/sri_trends_report_2005.pdf), pp. 19, 22.

4. Kevin Kelleher, "A Proxy Battle: Shareholders vs. CEOs," Corp-Watch, June 13, 2006 (www.corpwatch.org/article.php?id=13716).

5. "Record Year for Proxy Season," Social Investment Forum, October 2, 2006 (www.socialinvest.org/RecordYearforProxySeason.htm).

6. Michael C. Jensen and Richard S. Ruback, "The Market for Corporate Control: The Scientific Evidence," *Journal of Financial Economics* 11, nos. 1–4 (April 1983), pp. 5–50.

7. Aigbe Akhigbe, Jeff Madura, and Alan L. Tucker, "Long-Term Valuation Effects of Shareholder Activism," *Applied Financial Economics* 7, no. 5 (October 1, 1997), pp. 567–573.

8. See, e.g., Claire E. Crutchley, Carl D. Hudson, and Marlin R. H. Jensen, "Shareholder Wealth Effects of CalPERS' Activism," *Financial Services Review* 7, no. 1, 1998, pp. 1–10. Wilshire Associates has published a series of studies since 1994 examining "The CalPERS Effect." The latest update, by Andrew Junkin and Thomas Toth, "The 'CalPERS Effect' on Targeted Company Share Prices," July 27, 2006, is available online at www.calpersgovernance.org/alert/selection/WilshireRpt.pdf.

9. Junkin and Toth, "The 'CalPERS Effect,'" p. 9.

10. Jeremy Quittner, "Cracker Barrel Buckles," *The Advocate,* February 4, 2003.

11. Rule 14a-8(c)(7) of the Securities Exchange Act of 1934.

12. SEC No-Action Letter, "Cracker Barrel Old Country Store, Inc." (available October 13, 1992). See 17 C.F.R. § 240.14a-8(c)(7) (1994) ("Rule 14a-8(c)(7)").

13. SEC Release No. 34-40018 (May 21, 1998).

14. Data from "The State of the Workplace: 2000" and "The State of the Workplace: 2006," Human Rights Campaign (www.hrc.org).

15. Quittner, "Cracker Barrel Buckles."

16. Social Investment Forum, *2005 Report,* p. 25.

17. These examples are taken from the JPMorgan Chase & Co. 2006 proxy statement, "Notice of 2006 Annual Meeting of Shareholders and Proxy Statement," March 31, 2006 (http://files.shareholder.com/downloads/ONE/70837277x0x34667/80D316D7-6E75-4E9C-BDE2-7D4BB38FF998/2006_percent20proxy.pdf).

18. Jim Morris, "Power Trips: Privately Sponsored Trips Hot Tickets on Capitol Hill," Center for Public Integrity, June 5, 2006 (www.publicintegrity.org/powertrips/report.aspx?aid=799).

19. R. Jeffrey Smith, "DeLay Seeks New Judge for Texas Trial," *The Washington Post,* October 22, 2005 (www.washingtonpost.com/wp-dyn/content/article/2005/10/21/AR2005102100777.html).

Notes

20. See Social Investment Forum, *2005 Report,* p. 19, and Social Investment Forum, "Record Year for Proxy Season," October 2, 2006.

21. "Vote results" data provided by Center for Political Accountability (www.politicalaccountability.net/content.asp?contentid=426).

22. Center for Political Accountability, *The Green Canary,* February 15, 2005, pp. 28–29, 41–47 (www.politicalaccountability.net/files/GreenCanaryFinalA.pdf). The two companies were Morgan Stanley and AstraZeneca.

23. Ibid., pp. 41–47. The three companies were Morgan Stanley, Time Warner, and Exxon Mobil.

24. Ibid., pp. 49–54.

25. See Center for Political Accountability, *Hidden Rivers,* May 15, 2006 (www.politicalaccountability.net/files/HR06.pdf).

26. Jim VandeHei, "Political Cover: Major Business Lobby Wins Back Its Clout by Dispensing Favors," *The Wall Street Journal,* September 11, 2001, p. A1.

27. Peter H. Stone, "New Channels for Campaign Cash," *National Journal,* February 23, 2002, cited in Public Citizen, "Complaint to the U.S. Internal Revenue Service," October 31, 2006.

28. Laurie Beacham, "The Secret Chamber," Center for Justice & Democracy, July 2006 (www.centerjd.org/private/papers/Secret chamberstudy.pdf).

29. Public Citizen, "Complaint to the U.S. Internal Revenue Service," p. 15.

30. Center for Political Accountability, *The Green Canary,* p. 5.

31. Ibid., pp. 13–19.

32. Stanley Holmes, "Boeing: What Really Happened," *BusinessWeek,* December 15, 2003.

33. Ibid.

34. Marianne Brun-Rovet, Joshua Chaffin, Caroline Daniel, and James Harding, "Boeing's Skillful Lobbying Efforts," *Financial Times,* December 8th, 2003.

35. Center for Political Accountability, *The Green Canary,* pp. 22–23.

36. Poll conducted for the Center for Political Accountability by Mason-Dixon Polling & Research in March 2006. Results available at www.politicalaccountability.net.

37. List current as of March 1, 2007, courtesy of the Center for Political Accountability (www.politicalaccountability.net).

38. Richard Dunham, "A Mutual Fund That Plays Politics," *Business-Week,* February 5, 2007.

39. Powell, "Attack on American Free Enterprise System."

8. THE BLUEPRINT

1. Bill Berkowitz, "Richard Viguerie: Still Thundering After All These Years," *Working for Change,* March 4, 2005, www.working forchange.com/article.cfm?itemid=18669.

2. Christopher Hayes, "The New Funding Heresies," *In These Times,* July 2006, p. 31.

3. Tim Dickinson, "Can These Crashers Save This Party?" *San Francisco Magazine,* May 2006.

4. Daniel Terdiman, "ActBlue Lets Anyone Be PAC Man," *Wired,* September 28, 2004.

5. ActBlue press release, "Democratic Senators' Secret Weapon," November 6, 2006 (www.actblue.com/content/PR-senators-secret-weapon).

6. Kevin Phillips, *Wealth and Democracy: A Political History of the American Rich* (New York: Broadway Books, 2002), p. xiii.

7. "Wealth and Philanthropy: The Business of Giving," *The Economist,* February 23, 2006.

8. Jeff Krehely, Meaghan House, and Emily Kernan, "Axis of Ideology: Conservative Foundations and Public Policy," March 2004.

9. Hayes, "The New Funding Heresies," p. 29.

10. Robert G. Kaiser and Ira Chinoy, "Scaife: Funding Father of the Right," *The Washington Post,* May 2, 1999 (www.washingtonpost.com/wp-srv/politics/special/clinton/stories/scaifemain050299.htm). MediaTransparency (www.mediatrans

parency.org) has details of grants made to major right-wing institutions, including those from the Sarah Scaife Foundation.

11. The Brookings Institution, "Founding Ideals" (www.brookings
.edu/lib/founding.htm).

12. Jerome Armstrong and Markos Moulitsas Zúniga, *Crashing the
Gate: Netroots, Grassroots, and the Rise of People-Powered Politics*
(White River Junction, Vt.: Chelsea Green Publishing Co., 2006),
p. 70.

13. See MediaTransparency (www.mediatransparency.org) for details
of grants to the Cato Institute and the Institute on Religion and
Public Life, publisher of *First Things.*

14. Michael Crowley, "Growing Pains: The GOP Purge," *The New
Republic,* September 4, 2006.

15. Simon Rosenberg, "The Immigration Battle: Much to Be Proud
of, Much to Do," NDN, November 15, 2006 (www.ndnblog.org/
?q=node/483).

16. See Ari Berman, "Big $$ for Progressive Politics," *The Nation,*
October 16, 2006.

17. Ibid.

18. Andy Rappaport describes the venture capital mind-set of the
NPC in Dickinson, "Can These Crashers Save the Party?"

9. THE PROGRESSIVE ECOSYSTEM

1. Matt Bai, "The Multilevel Marketing of the President," *The New
York Times Magazine,* April 25, 2004.

2. Ibid.

3. Based on "reach" figures from Alexa (www.alexa.com), November
10, 2006.

4. See Chris Bowers and Matthew Stoller, "The Emergence of the
Progressive Blogosphere: A New Force in American Politics,"
New Politics Institute, August 10, 2005 (www.newpolitics.net/
node/87).

5. See Ori Brafman and Rod A. Beckstrom, *The Starfish and the Spider* (New York: Portfolio, 2006).

6. Jim Collins, *Good to Great* (London: Random House, 2001), chap. 2.

7. Jim Collins, *Good to Great and the Social Sectors* (London: Random House, 2006) pp. 10–11 (italics his).

8. Ibid., p. 12 (italics his).

9. Jerome Armstrong and Markos Moulitsas Zúniga, *Crashing the Gate* (White River Junction, Vt.: Chelsea Green Publishing Co., 2006), p. 123.

10. Mobile Voter Web site (http://mobilevoter.org).

11. The Pew Research Center's report "Luxury or Necessity?," December 14, 2006, found that 74 percent of Americans own a cell phone and 49 percent consider it a necessity. See http://pewresearch.org/pubs/323/luxury-or-necessity.

12. Sandra L. Suárez, "Mobile Democracy: Text Messages, Voter Turnout, and the 2004 Spanish General Election," presented at the American Political Science Association, September 2005 (http://electionupdates.caltech.edu/suarez.pdf).

13. Young Voter Strategies, "Young Voter Turnout Up for the Second Major Election in a Row," November 9, 2006 (www.youngvoter strategies.org/ index.php?tg=articles&idx=More&topics=37&article=282).

14. See Jill Lawrence, "Top Vote Counter Becomes Prize Job," *USA Today,* August 17, 2006.

15. Jeffrey R. Makin, *Are Ballot Propositions Spilling Over onto Candidate Elections?* Initiative and Referendum Institute Report 2006-2, October 2006 (www.iandrinstitute.org/REPORT%202006-2%20 Spillovers.pdf).

16. See the Initiative & Referendum Institute Report cited above for a summary of academic studies of the 2004 marriage initiatives.

17. Swindell, "Democrats Look to Trim GOP's Initiative Lead."

18. BISC, "Initiative Myths and Facts 2006," February 01, 2007, at www.ballot.org.

19. Kathleen Craig, "Why 'Unconferences' Are Fun Conferences," *Business 2.0 Magazine,* June 6, 2006 (money.cnn.com/2006/06/05/technology/business2_unconference0606/).

20. RootsCamp Frequently Asked Questions, rootscamp.pbwiki.com/FAQ.

21. Simon Rosenberg, "New Tools: Speak in Spanish," New Politics Institute, October 23, 2006 (www.newpolitics.net/node/180).

22. Progressive Majority, "Who We Are" (www.progressivemajority.org/whoweare/).

23. The Nation Blog, "Most Valuable Progressives of 2006" (www.thenation.com/blogs/thebeat?pid=152347).

24. Brad deGraf, "Smart Mobs vs. Amway," AlterNet, May 6, 2004 (www.alternet.org/story/18605/).

10. BLUE AMERICA

1. Jeffrey M. Jones, "Democratic Edge in Partisanship in 2006 Evident at National, State Levels," Gallup News Service, January 30, 2007 (galluppoll.com/content/default.aspx?ci=26308).

2. Ibid. The Gallup Organization does not poll in Alaska or Hawaii, which is why the states add up to only 48.

3. Stephanie Strom, "What's Wrong with Profit?" *The New York Times,* November 13, 2006.

4. Carlye Adler, "Can Corporations Save the World?" *Forbes,* November 28, 2006.

5. Mark Kramer and John Kania, "Changing the Game: Leading Corporations Switch from Defense to Offense in Solving Global Problems," *Stanford Social Innovation Review,* Spring 2006, p. 24.

6. "Face Value: The Shy Architect," *The Economist,* January 11, 2007.

Acknowledgments

The Blue Way—not unlike the organizations it describes—benefited from the tireless efforts, the intellectual resources, and the creativity of many kindred spirits.

There are many friends and colleagues to thank, but none more than Joel Hafvenstein, without whom this book simply would not have been possible. Joel's insights have made each and every page come alive. Joel—we are all greatly indebted to you for your help and your many talents.

Thank you also to Neeraja Bhavaraju, who brought together the wide-ranging quantitative and qualitative research that underlies the message of *The Blue Way*. Her broad understanding of corporate ethics and her passion for the progressive cause were instrumental in shaping every chapter. We are grateful to the immensely talented Dr. Jim Crooks, who not only performed many of the statistical analyses contained in this book but also helped everyone on the "blue team" understand their significance and relevance to the real-world management techniques we sought to describe. Thank you to Brett McCallum, who helped edit several of the early chapters. To Buck Owen, we

Acknowledgments

owe a debt of gratitude for his powerful insights into the world of Democratic fund-raising and nonprofit organizations.

For her insightful comments on the many versions of our manuscript and her commitment to our broader work together, thank you to Anne Slaughter Andrew. And to Athena Theodoro, for her unflinching support, our heartfelt appreciation.

Thank you also to our agent, Gail Ross, for her confidence and faith in our ideas. Finally, not least, a special thanks to our editor, Bob Bender, who never failed to remind us what *The Blue Way* was all about.

Last, thank you to all the progressive executives who make their companies "blue" and in so doing make our country a better place. They exemplify the premise of *The Blue Way*: you can profit by investing in a better world.

Index

Index

Index

Index

Index

Index

Printed in the United States
By Bookmasters